The OIQ Factor

Raising your school's
organizational intelligence

by William Powell and Ochan Kusuma-Powell

A John Catt Publication

First Published 2013

by John Catt Educational Ltd,
12 Deben Mill Business Centre, Old Maltings Approach,
Melton, Woodbridge IP12 1BL

Tel: +44 (0) 1394 389850 Fax: +44 (0) 1394 386893
Email: enquiries@johncatt.com
Website: www.johncatt.com

ISBN: 978 1 908095 91 6

eISBN: 978 1 908095 92 3

Set and designed by John Catt Educational Limited

Printed and bound in Great Britain
by Charlesworth Press

Contents

For Sean, Gulay, Colin and Jenny –
and the next generation of teachers
who will unquestionably raise the
organizational intelligence of schools.

Acknowledgements

Many people have contributed to this book. Ochan and Bill would specifically like to thank the Thinking Collaborative Community for its support, particularly our old friend and mentor, Bob Garmston.

We would also like to thank our colleagues of the Next Frontier Inclusion Design Team, Kevin Bartlett and Kristen Pelletier for rich conversations in the French Pyrenees where many ideas collided and connected.

Special thanks to Graham Mercer, Nick Bowley and Kevin Bartlett for reviewing the African Survival Simulation and contributing ideas and correcting mistakes.

And finally a word of appreciation to all the teachers in the scores of international schools that we work in each year. It is the greatest privilege and pleasure to learn with you.

Bill and Ochan Powell
Massat, France
May 2013

Preface

Who is this book for?

Many, perhaps even most, educational systems have got school improvement wrong. The authorities attempt to address the issue as a technical challenge. They are simplistic in their approach and often perceive schools as machines in need of repair or factories to be re-tooled. So the politicians and bureaucrats tinker with league tables, new curricular models and merit pay for teachers, spend vast amounts money, make a great deal of noise, and ultimately have little or no positive impact.

Schools are extremely complex organizations, in part because we invest in them our most precious assets – our children. Unlike businesses or commercial enterprises, schools have a multitude of success indicators, some of which are extremely difficult to quantify and may be time delayed by many years.

Simplistic and superficial approaches to improving student learning simply don't work because school improvement isn't a *technical* challenge; it is an *adaptive* one. It requires a change not just in behaviors and skills, but in values, beliefs and even identity. In a results-oriented age, impatient and frustrated school reformers may perceive this approach as a 'soft' option. However, any review of outstanding and improving schools will clearly demonstrate that high quality student learning is tied to school cultures that embrace learning for all. Raising organizational intelligence is all about re-culturing schools.

More than 20 years ago, Roland Barth (1990) wrote that school improvement is an inside-out process. It needs to come from within the school itself, from teachers and school leaders. More recently, Michael Fullan (2001) wrote that we don't need school reform or re-structuring, we need school re-culturing. School re-culturing is an internal process that cannot be mandated or imposed from outside.

Robert Garmston (2012) opens his recent book by asking the question: 'What dynamics have enabled some schools to become islands of optimism?' (p1) What forces conspire to allow some schools to develop a collective sense of responsibility for student learning? What conditions contribute to that collective efficacy that is so evident in some of our most effective schools?

The answer to these and many other questions relating to high quality and improving schools comes to reside in transformational learning – the type of learning that makes schools more collectively intelligent; more cognitively, socially and emotionally smart. This book is for teachers and school leaders who are looking for ways to raise the organizational intelligence quotient (OIQ) of their classrooms and their schools.

What does a school with a high OIQ factor look like? First of all, it is a place where teachers and students want to be. The buildings hum with activity seven days a week: athletes practice; musicians rehearse; actors memorize their lines and the yearbook staff work late hours to meet deadlines. The hum of activity is punctuated with laughter. Woven into the fabric of productivity is enjoyment.

In a school with high OIQ, teachers share a common sense of mission. They are intrinsically motivated and there is a culture of relational trust. They talk about "our" school and "our" students. Work and play become wonderfully confused. Territoriality is replaced by interdependence and accountability is second to responsibility. Teachers perceive themselves not as *learned*, but as *learning*.

Pride and humility walk hand in hand. Professional satisfaction runs high and yet there is no sense of complacency. Ideas are scrutinized in an atmosphere of respect and listening is valued at least as much as speaking. Leadership isn't rationed but is seen as a human right. There is positive peer group pressure, without insidious competition. The collective efficacy is contagious.

These are the schools we need and it is up to teachers to deliver them.

Politicians, the central office, even building principals by themselves cannot mandate transformative change. Teachers and school leaders must address such adaptive challenges. We need to reclaim our profession one school at a time.

Exploring organizational intelligence

The purpose of this book is to share with teachers and school leaders ways in which we can raise the organizational intelligence of classrooms and schools, but before we can look at the premises that underlie this book, we need to entertain two major propositions that may be foreign or at least strange to some readers.

The first proposition is that groups have distinct collective intelligence. There are smart teams and less smart teams and group intelligence is only weakly correlated to the individual intelligence of group members.

The second proposition is that collective intelligence is malleable. It can be enhanced and inhibited by the behaviors, attitudes, dispositions, and beliefs of the group members. In short, schools and school groups (grade level teams and subject area departments) have distinct collective intelligence. More significantly, organizational intelligence can be deliberately enhanced by teachers and school leaders, resulting in improved student and adult learning.

These two propositions run counter to much of the history of education where teaching was perceived as a solo act. There are some important premises that underlie the idea that every school can deliberately set out to improve and enhance its organizational intelligence.

Premise 1

Education is now too complex for individuals to go it alone. Asking teachers to fly solo is as out of date as the typewriter. In the past 20 years we have learned more about how the human brain learns than in all the rest of human history combined. We are in the midst of a renaissance in education and yet many schools are still using 19th century models and structures to address 21st century problems and issues. Many of these structures (*eg* the physical layout or the master schedule of classes) serve to isolate teachers and are impediments to improving collective intelligence.

Premise 2

Collective intelligence makes groups and organizations more effective, flexible, reflective and efficient; it also makes work more creative and fun. However, although the development of enhanced collective intelligence is unlikely to happen spontaneously or by default, it can be developed by design. Trust is the bedrock of organizational intelligence.

Premise 3

The skills of collaborative inquiry enhance organizational intelligence, but need to be taught explicitly. In order to raise the collective intelligence of a school, leadership needs to be redefined and distributed.

We believe that teachers and school leaders can influence collective intelligence and the chapters of the book reflect those influences: teacher leadership; emotional intelligence; contact architecture (our perceptions and management of space and time); professional collaboration; inclusion of children with special needs and stages of school development. At the conclusion of each chapter we have provided guided study questions, activities, simulations and case studies that illustrate key concepts.

This book is for teachers and other school leaders who perceive themselves as the facilitators of learning – for students, for colleagues and for themselves. If schools are to be transformed and transformative, teacher-learners will lead the way. That is how meaningful change has always happened. Only learners can raise the organizational intelligence of classrooms and schools.

Chapter 1

What is the OIQ factor?

Let's examine the organization intelligence of two very different schools.

The International School of Tanganyika

The International School of Tanganyika in Dar es Salaam, Tanzania, was a curious phenomenon. It was a school in which the collective intelligence of the organization appeared to be higher than the average individual intelligence of its teachers and administrators. Fewer than 20% of the faculty had advanced degrees and many of the teachers were young and short on experience. What they lacked in experience they made up for in enthusiasm, idealism and a sense of adventure.

The school was located in one of the poorest African countries with poor facilities. Until recently, classrooms were not air-conditioned. In the 1980s and '90s there was almost daily load shedding of electricity and frequent shortages of water. Gasoline was rationed and staple foodstuffs were in chronic short supply. Yet the hardships seemed to actually bring the faculty together into a sense of community.

Between 1979 and 1999, school leaders knew they could not use the meager salary that was on offer to attract teachers, so they focused on creating professional learning opportunities and promoting teachers to positions of responsibility from within the school. The school encouraged co-teaching and reflective practice and developed numerous initiatives to share expertise, including small innovative teaching grants and annual research fellowships.

For three years, the teachers wrote, edited, and published an annual professional journal entitled *Finding Our Voices: A Journal of Effective Teaching Practice*. A spirit of professional optimism and efficacy pervaded.

The school had an inclusive admissions policy, an extensive learning support unit and, at the same time, outstanding International Baccalaureate examination results. It sent its graduates to the finest universities worldwide. It also had a scholarship program for host country nationals and an extensive community service program.

Years later, teachers who had worked at the International School of Tanganyika during this time recalled their tenure there as a 'renaissance' or 'golden age'. Almost 50 teacher alumni of this school went on to become directors or principals of major international schools around the world and to senior leadership positions in organizations such as the International Baccalaureate, the European Council of International Schools and the Association of International Schools in Africa.

Curiously, the International School of Tanganyika combined a fairly high OIQ factor with a pervasive inferiority complex. It was actually a much better school than it thought it was.

The International School of the Andaman Sea

Several years ago we were both invited to a large international school in Asia (we'll call it the International School of the Andaman Sea [ISAS]), to conduct a workshop on assessment in the differentiated classroom. By the coffee break on the first morning, we had independently reached the conclusion that something was very wrong. During the break, we talked with individual participants about their school in an attempt to understand the apparent resistance and unusually widespread defensiveness that they demonstrated.

We heard from the staff that the school was one of the very best in Asia, perhaps even the world. We heard that 20% of the teachers had doctorates and another 60% had masters' degrees. It was a very bright and highly experienced faculty. The Headmaster prided himself on his recruiting skills: "I only hire the superstars," he said.

Accordingly ISAS had a history of respectable IB examination results and its graduates gained admission to selective universities. Parents considered ISAS to be the school of choice for university entrance and placement. In short, ISAS was already perceived to be a success story and a good number of the teachers didn't understand why they had been asked to attend a workshop on differentiation.

In fact, one teacher suggested that he was actually offended that the administration had organized such a workshop. "There's implied criticism. The admin are saying that I don't know how to do my job. It's like I'm being retreaded or something." One teacher asked: "Why can't the administration just leave us alone to get on with what we have been trained to do?"

Another teacher asked: "Are we really doing kids a favor by making learning easy for them?" Still another commented: "Where are the administration? They organize a workshop and then don't attend themselves. If they have something better to do, then so do we!"

A portrait of an arrogant, unhappy and mistrustful school culture emerged. Teachers were for the most part isolated from each other. There was a spirit of competitiveness between and amongst faculty and there was little collaboration or sharing of craft knowledge. There was no peer coaching or mentoring; in fact, the opposite was the case. Many teachers considered the unit plans they had developed to be private intellectual property. One teacher had developed a series of rubrics for different forms of expository writing, but refused to share them with colleagues until the school purchased the rights from her.

A substantial number of the teachers had been at the school for more than 20 years. Newer and younger teachers didn't tend to stay much beyond their initial two-year contract. They had trouble settling in and several reported that they didn't feel accepted by the more established faculty members. One veteran teacher said that he was feeling very frustrated with the new teachers who came in each year expecting their ideas to be treated seriously. "The new teachers' ideas just don't have as much value as those of us who have been here for a long time. We have the experience. We know the ropes."

When the teachers did get together, their interaction with each other and the administration were often characterized by competiveness, rudeness and sarcasm. It was tacitly accepted practice to interrupt and put down colleagues. There was a sense of one-upmanship. The high school principal had been reduced to public tears in two recent faculty meetings and the elementary principal had all but stopped holding faculty meetings.

One of the newer teachers mentioned quietly: "While we get pretty good exam results, we don't place our kids into the most selective universities. Something's going on here. The school isn't a happy place. I wouldn't want my child in this high school. I'll be looking for another assignment after this contract."

The irony of the International School of the Andaman Sea is that, while it was unquestionably staffed with extremely intelligent and experienced teachers, it was not an intelligent school. The collective organizational intelligence was far below the average individual intelligence of its members. It had a toxic culture. The potential that it had for collective creativity and innovation was not realized because of a prevailing culture of competition, suspicion and mistrust.

Perhaps the greatest irony was that ISAS was unable to see itself as it really was. But, someone might argue, ISAS had respectable IB results and university placements. If we are results orientated, how can we think of ISAS as other than successful?

An excellent question: one that brings us to one of the major premises of this book. We believe that schools with high organizational intelligence are values-driven. They are idealistic and live their beliefs and values on a daily basis. Strong standardized test scores are important, but they must be seen as a *symptom* or *desirable by-product* of a healthy school.

ISAS was examination-results driven. It determined its success, not by its values and beliefs, but by it's bottom line – standardized test scores. Enron and the Atlanta school district have taught us all too well what happens when numbers eclipse values – cheating becomes rife.

Schools have organizational intelligence

When groups of people come together for a common purpose, they form organizations that develop different degrees of collective intelligence quotients. Organizations, like people, have measureable intelligence. There are smart organizations that capitalize on the individual creativity and innovation of their members and there are less intelligent organizations that squander or ignore the talents of their members. Smart organizations develop collective intelligence that far exceeds the average individual intelligence of its members.

What does organizational intelligence look like in practice? We have all witnessed high performing groups and groups that were dysfunctional. The difference was not the individual intelligence of group members, but the collective smarts of the team working together. Smart groups are able to make sense out of a mass of data, distinguishing the relevant from the merely tangential. They organize and integrate knowledge more thoroughly; plan more carefully; and anticipate more accurately the consequences of their decisions and actions.

Smart groups are socially sensitive and have considerable political acumen. They are more efficient in their work; they do more work in less time and expend less effort. Groups that have high collective intelligence are more innovative, more likely to find creative solutions to problems, more likely to engage in reflection and therefore more likely to transfer their learnings to new and novel situations.

Like individual intelligence (Nisbett 2009), organizational intelligence is malleable. We can make our collective selves smarter.

Two heads are not necessarily better than one
There are two prevailing falsehoods in the field of organizational intelligence. These myths focus on both quantity and quality. The first falsehood is that 'two heads are better than one'.

Two minds can indeed be better than one, but it is not necessarily so. The quantity of minds is not correlated to collective intelligence. You can have large and small stupid groups. The critical variable is how those two or more minds interact together.

The second falsehood is even more prevalent and demonstrably inaccurate: that by getting very bright people together to work on the same task, we will create a highly effective group. In other words we will raise our organization's intelligence. This has been shown to be false time and time again. The quality of the individual minds that comprise the group is only weakly correlated to enhanced collective intelligence (Malone 2010).

A high degree of organizational intelligence depends greatly on paying attention not just to *what* people do, but *how* they do it together. High organizational intelligence produces synergy – when the product of group effort greatly exceeds the sum of individual accomplishments.

Considerable research has been undertaken recently on organizational intelligence. However, little has been applied directly to work in schools. An exception is the work of Robert Garmston. Garmston (2012) points out that the attributes that make groups more effective (smarter) are NOT the factors that most people might suppose would make groups work better. Factors such as group satisfaction, group cohesion and group motivation actually have little influence on collective intelligence and effectiveness.

The knowledge paradox

Perhaps one of the greatest paradoxes organizations face in striving to enhance collective intelligence is the tension between recognizing that knowledge is of great value, and then asking individuals and groups to voluntarily share it with others. How many times have we heard people in high places exhort us that 'knowledge is power'? On the surface, freely sharing knowledge would seem to run counter to human nature.

Except of course that we are focused on the organizational intelligence of schools and it is the mission of schools to be places of learning where knowledge *is* shared freely. And yet, even with that said, knowledge management in schools remains to a large extent in the Stone Age.

Schools are organizations that specialize in learning and, as such, should be very smart organizations. Frequently, however, they're not. High organizational intelligence in school improves student learning, raises standardized test scores, enhances the professional satisfaction of teachers and administrators, reduces work related stress and increases parent confidence in the school.

However, high organizational intelligence in schools rarely happens by chance. In fact, we would argue vigorously that it is far too important to be left to chance. It can be developed by design. This book is about how teachers and school leaders can deliberately set about raising the OIQ factor in an increasingly interdependent world.

Smart people and stupid decisions

History is replete with examples of how very intelligent people have come together to make stupid decisions. Barbara Tuchman, in her book, *The*

March of Folly (1984), chronicles how human history has been full of cohorts of the best and the brightest men (and they were usually *men*) of their generation coming together to make decisions that would lead to fairly predictable small and large catastrophes. From the fall of Troy to the defeat of the Inca nation; from King George III losing the American colonies; to the debacle of the Vietnam War; Tuchman describes recurring instances of abysmal organizational intelligence. Unfortunately schools are not immune from such collective simplemindedness.

For organizations to be intelligent it is not enough to fill them with intelligent people. The OIQ factor requires that we examine how people actually work together.

Our propensity to work in groups
From our pre-history in the Magdalenian caves of southern France, one of the defining features of humankind has been our propensity to work in groups. Arguably one of the most powerful ideas driving our evolution and development as a species is the limit to what one individual can achieve on his or her own.

Accordingly, groups of individuals came together to pursue the common objective of survival. In fact, recent research in neuroscience suggests that we may be biologically hard-wired to be social creatures (Iacaboni 2009). In these pre-historic hunting, foraging and later agricultural groups we see the genesis of modern organizations. The collective was for the most part more powerful, effective and productive than the individual. From the advent of spoken language some 50,000 years ago, conversation has been the means though which we have collectively organized ourselves.

> *Since our earliest ancestors gathered in circles around the warmth of a fire, conversation has been our primary means for discovering what we care about, sharing knowledge, imagining the future and acting together to both survive and thrive... Conversation is our human ways of creating and sustaining or transforming – the realities in which we live.*

> Brown and Issacs, 2005

The Industrial Revolution and the emergence of the factory assembly line gave us the metaphor of the organizational *machine*. We assumed that human organizations could be likened to a machine, with a clear purpose, discrete parts, with input and output and a means to measure efficiency and productivity. When all the parts of the machine were working, the machine was productive, goods were manufactured and the outcome was a healthy balance sheet. There was a pleasant, common sense simplicity to the model.

The comfortable predictability of Newtonian physics could be seen in human organizations. The epitome of the machine metaphor was the theory of Scientific Management as formulated by Frederick Winslow Taylor. Taylorism held that the acid test of an organization was its efficiency and productivity. He also had some fairly rigid ideas about how it should be implemented. He wrote:

> It is only through *enforced* standardization of methods, *enforced* adoption of the best implements and working conditions, and *enforced* cooperation that this faster work can be assured. And the duty of enforcing the adoption of standards and enforcing this cooperation rests with *management* alone.

> Taylor cited in Montgomery 1989, p 229, italics with Taylor.

Taylor's vision of Scientific Management is still very much with us today and the beliefs that form its foundation keep many organizations, including schools, collectively stupid.

When applied to education, the underlying assumption of Taylorism is that teachers, if left to their own devices, will only do the bare minimum and that in order to achieve anything more, management needs to practice coercive leadership. In other words, there is the prevalence of the belief that the goal of leadership is teacher compliance and this compliance in schools can be achieved through the use of rewards and punishments – the positive and negatives reinforcements.

There are numerous faulty assumptions here. The first is that teaching and learning can be reduced to a single set of standards and practices to which all teachers must adhere. There are indeed principles of good teaching practice, but once these have been reduced to algorithmic behaviors, they lose most, if not all their efficacy and meaningfulness.

The second faulty assumption is that highly cognitive and creative labor, such as teaching, can be motivated by extrinsic rewards and punishments. Research points to the direct opposite: that extrinsic rewards, such as financial bonus or merit pay, actually inhibit cognitive labor (Pink 2009).

Scientific Management has been attempted time and again and the approach simply doesn't work for any endeavor that requires thought and creativity. The assumptions of Scientific Management are based on thinking about schools as machines. We can see the impact of the machine metaphor in all externally enforced attempts at reform, such as the No Child Left Behind or the Race to the Top initiatives in the United States.

We also see the machine metaphor in recent attempts to tie student results on standardized tests to the evaluation and remuneration of teachers. In addition, Taylor's condescension is still with us in efforts by the central office to produce 'teacher proof' curricular documents.

Schools as living organisms

There are many problems with the machine metaphor, but perhaps the most telling is that it doesn't provide for self-organizing development, sustainability or self-directedness. This is the central thesis of Arie De Geus' book, *The Living Company* (1997).

For many years, De Geus was the coordinator of worldwide planning for Royal Dutch Shell and led a fascinating research project. De Geus and his team looked at how long Fortune 500 companies survive. To his surprise, he discovered that the average life expectancy for Fortune 500 companies (those companies that are at the very top of their game) was only 40 to 50 years.

De Geus surmised that the majority of these companies die prematurely because they have learning disabilities. In other words, they fail to adapt and evolve to the changing environment; they have a low OIQ factor. 'Companies die because their managers focus on the economic activity of producing goods and services, and they forget that their organization's true nature is that of a community of humans' (p3). In other words, the premature death of these organizations is the result of the machine metaphor.

One of the key ideas that emerges from De Geus' work is that the profitability of a company is a *symptom* of corporate health, but not a *predictor* or *determinant* of corporate health. When profitability determines corporate health we have the machine metaphor. When profitability is a desirable by-product of corporate health we have a living, sustainable organization.

Schools often quantify their success by way of standardized examination and test results. We also hear this frequently when IB Diploma teachers justify their resistance to new ideas and innovation with the comment, "my kids are getting good examination results".

Let's go back to the International School of the Andaman Sea. You will recall that it had strong IB results and sent its graduates to selective universities. Let's substitute the ideas of standardized examination scores (IB results) and admissions to prestigious universities for the concept of 'profitability'. De Geus would probably tell us that outstanding examination results do NOT determine a school's success or predict a school's health.

This was certainly the case with the ISAS (good examination results are relatively easy to achieve if you have a selective admissions policy). In healthy schools all members of the community are engaged in learning (not just the students) and that learning reflects a much broader spectrum than can be measured on a standardized test.

We reject the simplistic, formulaic notion that 'good results=good schools'. Good schools are more than that. A good school is a living community in which relationships are nurtured and everyone is included, challenged and successful.

Seeing a school as a living entity means that the values and beliefs that lie at the heart of the school's culture and ethos are what humanizes the present and provides a vision for the future. Peter Senge writes,

> Seeing a company as a machine implies that its members are employees or, worse, 'human resources', humans standing in reserve, waiting to be used. Seeing a company as a living being leads to seeing its members as human work communities (in de Geus, *The Living Company*. pIX, 1997).

Perhaps the most important distinction between our metaphors of 'machine' and 'living entity' comes to the forefront when we look at learning. Machines can't learn. They can be programmed and reprogrammed, but they cannot learn or adapt themselves to their environment. They can only repeat processes for which they have been designed. Only living beings can learn. School communities should be places of robust learning for all members.

What is the OIQ factor?

Organizations have collective intelligence. There are creative and imaginative organizations and fairly staid and traditional ones. Like individual people, organizations can exhibit flashes of brilliance and, at times, all the attributes of crass stupidity. They may fail to detect even the most obvious signals of change in the environment.

For example, the Swiss watch industry came perilously close to oblivion when it failed to recognize the worldwide movement to digital timepieces. Smith Corona was so focused on improving their typewriters that they failed to perceive that the world was moving to personal computers. The pursuit of excellence is not enough. The last typewriter Smith Corona ever produced was unquestionably its best – but it was also its last. In 1995 Smith Corona declared bankruptcy.

Organizations with low OIQ factors may fail to respond appropriately – or at all – to the most insistent demands of stakeholders. These organizations learn slowly, making the same mistakes repeatedly without gaining insight or increased understanding. Stupidity is not making a mistake: it is making the same mistake over and over again. Intelligent people become easily frustrated in stupid organizations.

Karl Albrecht (2003) formulated what he refers to as Albrecht's law: 'Intelligent people, when assembled into an organization, will tend towards collective stupidity' (p4). Although not inevitable, it is a disturbingly common pattern. Albrecht perceives leadership as the key to determining organizational intelligence.

What does high collective intelligence look like?

Sometimes it is useful to think of something in terms of what it is not. Organizational intelligence is NOT the abrogation of individual intelligence. It is not groupthink in which the premature desire for group cohesion eclipses critical thinking. Collective intelligence is when we maximize the intelligence of the individual through the process of the group and achieve collectively what no one of us could have accomplished on our own.

A basic prerequisite of individual intelligence is consciousness of self, which is absent in lower order organisms. Because we have consciousness of self, we are fascinated by, perhaps even obsessed with, the idea of individual intelligence. As teachers, we spend a good portion of our waking hours every day recognizing, exploring and assessing individual intelligence. We do it daily in the classroom, in problem-solving meetings with colleagues, when we participate in a professional development workshop or when interviewing prospective employees.

We are constantly analyzing and evaluating the individual intelligence of other people. And while we may have considerable difficulty in articulating what exactly intelligence comprises, most of us are supremely self-confident that we can recognize its presence or absence in others.

Recognizing and evaluating collective intelligence in organizations is much less familiar to us and there are a number of reasons for this. It may be that the concept of organizational intelligence is foreign to us, or we may be so close to the organization that we can't see the forest for the trees. Or perhaps, as may have been the case with the International School of the Andaman Sea, predetermined prejudices and filters can interfere with and color perceptions.

We can grow more familiar with the concept of organizational intelligence by looking at the ways in which it is similar and different to individual intelligence.

Generally we recognize an intelligent individual as someone who has great skill in processing a complex mass of data and making sense from it; has a relatively large frame of reference and is able to make unusual but meaningful connections; has an exceptional ability to respond to complex situations appropriately; is able to fashion or create products; and has the ability to learn quickly.

Collective intelligence is similar to individual intelligence in that it is seen to be *transferable.* In other words, the group's collective ability on one set of tasks can help predict its results on others (Woolley *et al*, 2010). This is significant in the sense that intelligence is seen to be an emerging pattern of understood and agreed-to interactions that can be effective and productive in new and novel situations. Given the breakneck rate of change that we are experiencing, the predictive dimension of collective intelligence gives us much reason for optimism and hope.

If we can define organizational intelligence as the *emergence of understood and agreed to patterns of effective interaction,* then it makes sense that in smart schools, teachers pay close attention not only to *what* they are doing, but also *how* they are doing it. Both *product* and *process* receive close scrutiny. Teachers in intelligent schools are able to perceive both the forest and the trees; and distinguish between the path and the act of walking upon it.

They have a clear vision of the big picture and they communicate that vision clearly and frequently. Communicating the overarching vision of the school, its broad values and educational beliefs, breaks down the walls of provincialism and territoriality. However, the vision of the truly intelligent organization isn't limited to *what* we do, but includes *how* we go about doing it.

For the last several years, schools around the world have been developing so-called 'dashboards' of organization effectiveness and efficiency. Simply defined, a dashboard is an instrument to present data. One of the purposes of these dashboards is to provide boards of trustees and occasionally parents with a quick and simple way of monitoring the progress the school is making towards achieving its goals.

Such dashboards work reasonably well for educational features that can be easily quantified: enrollment statistics; budgets; construction projects; standardized test scores; university entrance results; *etc.* They are virtually useless for reporting on the elements of school culture that contribute to organizational intelligence, which are extremely difficult, if not impossible, to quantify. For example, the degree to which trust is present, the quality of relationships, the maturity of group collaboration or the extent of transformational adult learning.

The danger of dashboards is that so-called 'hard data', our obsession with numbers crowds out truly important, but less easy to measure, dimensions of high quality schools.

Each August or September, international school directors 'check in' on two electronic list serves: Headnet and AISHnet . The check in process usually involves a greeting to colleagues around the world, best wishes for the new school year, and brief paragraphs about the state of the individual school.

An informal survey undertaken in August 2012 found that over 80% of the Heads that checked in reported solely on enrollment and budget figures and new construction projects. Each is easily quantifiable. What we pay attention to is a clear indication of what we value.

The good news is that emerging research (Woolley *et al*, 2010) suggests that it is easier to raise the intelligence of a group than it is the intelligence of individuals. The bad news is that we must also presume that the opposite is also the case. It is easier to inhibit the intelligence of a group than it is that of an individual. If group intelligence is even more malleable than individual intelligence, the implications for learning organizations (and classrooms) are great and it behooves all educators to pay close attention not only to what groups do but also how they do their work.

We will look closely at the processes that highly intelligent groups employ in later chapters. However, at this point, both research and experience suggests that smart groups are self-consciously aware of their behavioral norms (they have developed essential agreements for how they will work together): leadership is distributed; group members are open to new ideas; trusting and respectful behavior is present; criticism is constructively focused on issues and ideas, not on individuals; and group members listen actively and reflectively to each other.

Teachers in intelligent schools are enthusiastic consumers of new knowledge. School leaders and faculty attempt to stay abreast of recent research and developments in the field. Members attend conferences, present workshops, read and discuss articles, and write for professional publications. Teachers are keen to discover what other colleagues may be engaged in as 'works in progress' and are eager to share and critique new ideas. In short, intelligent schools are inhabited by teachers who are learning and growing.

Smart organizations foster a climate of habitual curiosity and inquiry. There is a common expectation that new ideas will be shared, that initial judgment will be suspended and that rigorous scrutiny will occur within a respectful context of inquiry.

Teachers support the development of organizational intelligence by understanding the difference between a school's mission and its strategies. In other words, there is consistent connection to the school's deeply-held values, but flexibility in how the school goes about pursuing those goals.

For example, the mission statement of the International School of Brussels (ISB) is 'Everyone included, everyone challenged, everyone successful.'

The school serves a population of students that ranges from the very highly capable to those with intensive learning needs and ISB takes great pride in being inclusive; there is no deviation from the mission.

At the same time, there is constant appraisal and re-appraisal of the strategies that ISB employs to realize its mission. Smart schools welcome and, in fact, demand flexibility of thought. They are constantly asking themselves: is there another way we could look at this situation? Is there another interpretation that we might construct, another way to approach this child? Teachers in smart schools engage in empathy and see the world through many different lenses. Truly intelligent schools not only tolerate, but appreciate ambiguity.

Finally, truly intelligent schools learn quickly because they have learned collectively *how* to learn. Many schools around the world claim to teach students *to learn how to learn*. Few, in our experience, actually do so explicitly. When schools do explicitly teach children meta-cognitive strategies and learning skills (how to learn), something quite remarkable happens. Teachers and school leaders become more self-consciously aware of their own learning, and meta-cognition becomes woven into the fabric of the adult-to-adult relationships.

In short, schools with high OIQ factors hold three questions firmly in the forefront of their collective consciousness (Garmston & Wellman 2009): *Who are we? Why are we doing this? Why are we doing this this way?*

A common pattern in high quality and improving schools is to have pockets of collective teacher intelligence. The pockets often grow up spontaneously and organically as a result of the specific personal characteristics and attributes that teachers bring to a department or team. In such instances we see synergy, the interaction of two or more people so that their combined effect is greater than the sum of their individual effort. However, in most cases, such synergy is unplanned. It is the fortuitous result of having the right people in the right place at the right time. The proverbial 'chemistry' works.

Organizational intelligence is too important to be left to chance. All schools have the potential to design structures and implement strategies that will provide opportunities for synergy. All schools have the potential to raise the collective intelligence above that of the average individual.

Two flavors of collective stupidity

Experience suggests that collective stupidity comes in two flavors. Albrecht (2003) refers to these as 'Learned' and 'Designed-In'. Learned stupidity is when people believe they are not authorized to think. This is actually more common than any of us would like to acknowledge. Sometimes it is the product of an authoritarian culture; other times it is self-imposed.

For example, most of us would agree that the curriculum should be meaningful, relevant and respectful. It should not be merely an academic exercise that keeps children busy. Sometimes in our professional development workshops we ask upper elementary classroom teachers why they are teaching the multiplication and division of fractions (when did you last multiple or divide a fraction?). Many times, we receive a blank stare in response or the teacher may announce that multiplication and division of fractions are part of the curriculum. In other words, ours is not to reason why, just invert and multiply.

In many respects learned stupidity is related to learned helplessness. We often see this in schools with autocratic, paternal or coercive leadership that serves to dis-empower teachers. We also see it as a product of the frequent use of extrinsic rewards and punishment. It harks back to the operant conditioning of the Behaviorists. Recent research is clear that the use of extrinsic rewards and punishments can be effective in terms of physical labor, but is not so for cognitive labor (Pink, 2009).

Paying fruit pickers by the number of bushels of apples they collect at the end of the day appears to improve productivity. However, the use of such extrinsic rewards and punishments has a deleterious effect on cognitive labor. It inhibits thinking, creativity, collaboration, and intellectual risk-taking. It fosters 'learned' collective stupidity.

Many teachers have become so used to the constraints under which they work that they are simply not aware of them anymore. We often fail to understand that the future will not look like the past and we become seduced into complacency by current success. The old adage: 'the future has arrived; it is just not evenly distributed yet' is perhaps nowhere more true than in schools. Business as usual thinking is the enemy of creativity, learning and growth.

Designed-in stupidity exists when rules and regulations make it difficult or impossible for people to think creatively, constructively or independently. We see designed-in stupidity every time someone attempts to design a teacher-proof curriculum or when teachers are told that they are expected to collaborate but are not provided time, training or space to do so.

We also see designed-in stupidity when groups of individuals engage in what van der Heijden (2002) calls 'framing flaws' (p46). Framing flaws are interpretations of problems and issues from a single, myopic and often under-examined position. Van der Heijden suggests that the role we occupy will often influence the way that we see or understand a problem or issue.

For example, an international school in South America has just received its standardized test scores in literacy. The results show a significant decline in student literacy from the previous year. When the scores are disaggregated, the dip appears to be the product of students who are still in the process of learning English.

Different groups may see this issue through different lenses depending on their role within the school. The ESL teachers may see the results as a product of large class size and a lack of resources. The remedy? Hire more ESL teachers and purchase more resources. The administration may see the issue as a result of mainstream teachers being unfamiliar with the learning needs of ESL students. The remedy? More professional development. Some parents may see issue as a result of a revised admissions policy that is effectively lowering academic statements and inhibiting the achievement of non-ESL students. Our roles often contain vested self-interest and can influence the way we come to understand complex situations.

Our individual and collective psychological needs can also inhibit collective intelligence. Van der Heijden identifies three avoidance dimensions that individuals and groups can fall victim to. Each can limit the intelligent collective processing of information.

Error avoidance
The first dimension is error avoidance. This emerges when a group or team becomes aware that the strategy that they have embarked on may not be working in the manner they had hoped and predicted. Instead of

re-examining the strategy, admitting error and framing the problem or issue, the team simply 'doubles down' on it and escalates its commitment.

> Groups or individuals that make the initial decision tend to escalate their commitment to the decision despite negative feedback, whereas those that inherit decisions are less likely to do so. (p57)

We see this error avoidance frequently when simplistic solutions are applied to complex problems (*eg* evaluating teacher performance primarily through the use of standardized test scores.).

Perhaps one of the most significant historical cases of error avoidance was the obsessive commitment by the French military to Plan 17 – an offensive plan to defeat the German forces in World War One. The plan was an unmitigated disaster and cost hundreds of thousands of lives; however as evidence of its faults and flaws poured into the General Staff Headquarters, the top brass' commitment to the plan grew increasingly strong (Tuchman, 1962).

Uncertainty avoidance

The second dimension is the avoidance of uncertainty. Uncertainty makes many, perhaps most people, uncomfortable and we tend to avoid it by looking for evidence that will validate a pre-existing bias. Many times the evidence that we draw upon is either too narrow or simply flawed. Avoidance of uncertainty can take the form of either confirmation bias or hindsight bias.

One of the most commonly used examples of confirmation bias is the 'waiter paradox'. In this our waiter has been assigned too many tables to attend to with equally high standards of service. The waiter has many years' experience and believes he is masterful at distinguishing in advance between those customers who are big and small tippers.

Accordingly our waiter focuses his attention on the customers who he believes will tip well and ignores those that he believes will not. Over time, the waiter discovers that his strategy has worked well. He comes to believe he has real expertise in identifying those who will leave large tips.

The problem, of course, is that the larger tips may actually be a result of the better service provided. In order to actually validate his strategy, our waiter would need to provide inferior service to those he predicted to be large tippers and vice versa – something his self-preservation is unlikely to allow him to do. Nevertheless, there is real intellectual danger in being a 'naïve scientist' and assuming confirmation on a single piece of data.

The hindsight bias is another form of the avoidance of uncertainty. Psychological research (van der Heijden, 2002, p51-52) suggests that we have a tendency to downplay the predictions that we get wrong and exaggerate our more accurate predictions. In schools we see this when IB Diploma teachers are asked to develop predicted grades for students. If there is a sizeable discrepancy between the predicted grade and the actual exam result, our tendency is to claim that we had low confidence in the prediction and externalize the cause (home problems, erratic student effort, unfair or ambiguous exam questions).

However, if our predictions are accurate, we tend to claim high confidence in them. This can be a product of 'hindsight bias'. The danger here is that hindsight bias may preclude us from learning from experience. We may become subject to the 'I-knew-it-all-the time' syndrome.

> *In general, then, it would seem that we don't learn from experience because we believe that experience has little to teach us: our recollections of our judgmental predictions confirm these to have been accurate. We believe our judgments, predictions and choices are well made, but this confidence may be misplaced.* (p52)

Stress avoidance

Many complex situations that individuals and groups find themselves in produce large degrees of stress. In groups, stress manifests itself in anxiety, fear, irritation, impatience and often outright anger. These emotions are contagious (Hatfield, 1994). A group member may demonstrate stress and this may cause others in the group to share the stress emotions. Such stress is most frequently present when a group needs to make a decision that involves a degree of risk.

For example, a school may see a sudden decline in enrollment and the Board of Trustees may need to make some hard and unpopular decisions about managing expenses. Stress avoidance can take many forms. We see it when groups repeatedly procrastinate, vacillate, or pass the buck. Stress avoidance can seriously hinder collective intelligence. Groups need to identify stress-producing issues and actively discuss stress management strategies.

Enhancing our collective intelligence is about two things: avoiding collective stupidity and practicing behaviors than promote transformational learning. In the next chapter, we will examine how teacher leaders can promote such learning.

Guided study questions

Although the International School of the Andaman Sea has creditable IB examination results, the authors suggest that it was relatively low in organizational intelligence. What, specifically, do they mean by this?

What are some of the differences between a values-driven school and an examination-results driven school? What connections are you exploring to your own school?

What are some values that might drive a school that is attempting to raise its organizational intelligence?

In what situations have you encountered 'learned' or 'designed-in' stupidity?

Which departments or teams in your school exhibit high degrees of organizational intelligence? What might be some of the contributing factors?

African safari simulation

An exercise in developing collective intelligence
Background to the simulation
Below is a survival simulation set in the African bush. It provides groups with an opportunity to compare individual critical thinking to that of the group; analyze the process of decision-making that the group went through; and reflect upon the group dynamics. Ultimately it allows groups to identify how they enhanced (or on rare occasions inhibited) their organizational intelligence.

Directions for the facilitator
Organize the participants into groups of five or six. Read the 'situation' and the 'challenge' out loud to the whole group. Ask participants individually to rank the salvaged items. During the individual ranking there should be no consultation. Also ask the participants not to change their individual rankings once they are permitted to discuss the challenge with their teammates. Then provide teams with about 30 minutes to develop a team ranking. Provide participants with the 'experts' ranking' and have them score themselves both as individuals and as a team. Have the teams reflect on how they have developed collective intelligence by analyzing the scoring in steps 6-11.

The situation
You and a group of friends make a last minute decision to drive out of the city to the nearest game park and enjoy a weekend in the bush. You drive about 300 kilometers west of Dar es Salaam in East Africa to Mikumi National Park.

The road is pot holed and you drive carefully to avoid the many long haul trucks and buses. You arrive at Mikumi at 4pm and register at the Ranger Station. There is only one ranger on duty. He explains that the rest have gone to Dar es Salaam, taking all the park vehicles, for a week's training. You check into the tented camp and by 4.30pm you are in your Land Rover heading off for an early evening game drive.

The grassland on either side of the well-traveled tarmac road is dotted with herds of wildebeest, zebra, impala and buffalo. Grazing amid the baobab trees are small groups of elephants. You have spotted a seldom-used track on the south side of the tarmac road that leads up into some lovely acacia covered hills – ideal country for spotting lions and, if you're lucky, leopard. The Land Rover isn't air-conditioned and even in the late afternoon the tropical sun is merciless.

You follow the dirt track for about 35 kilometers, pausing periodically to photograph warthog, silver-backed jackal and a brilliant lilac-breasted roller. The road divides and you take the left fork. This is a track you have never been on before; in fact, you don't remember seeing it marked on the visitor's map of the park. Several times you have to roll up the windows because you pass through tsetse fly territory. You know that tsetse flies can carry sleeping sickness.

The track becomes less and less defined in the tall grass and you wonder if it's wise to continue. However, in the distance you spot a herd of Cape Buffalo. The photo-opportunity is irresistible. About 15 minutes later, you hear the deep coughing of a lion in scrub brush. You follow the sound.

After about ten more kilometers, you come to the crest of a steep hill that leads down to a valley and small stream. The track down is deeply rutted from recent rains. You steer the Land Rover so that its wheels stay on the crest of the ruts. You proceed slowly down the steep hill. About 20 meters further the left wheels slip into the rut.

You engage the four-wheel drive, low range, and attempt to reverse up the hill. All four tires spin in the loose earth. You turn the wheels to the right and try to go forward. The center of gravity shifts and the Land Rover rolls. The windscreen shatters and the roof collapses.

Your group climbs out of the Land Rover through the windows. No one is seriously hurt, although everyone is badly shaken.

You try your mobile phone, but there is no signal. Mikumi isn't covered by a cell phone network. You glance at your watch. It's now 5.30pm. Darkness will fall in about an hour-and-a-half. The Land Rover is inoperable, but you find a few things in the vehicle that may help sustain you.

Again you hear the cough of a lion. But this time it is much closer. You listen intently. Fear congeals in your gut and you wonder how you will survive.

The challenge
Your task is to rank the 12 items (listed below) that the members of your group have identified as potentially useful. Rank them according to their

importance to your survival, starting with a 1 for the most important to a 12 for the least important. You may assume that the number of people is the same as the number on your team.

Step one: Review the list of available items. Without discussing them with your team, rank these items in the order of their importance to your team's survival. Record your individual ranks in the column labeled Step one.

Step two: Now, as a team, reconsider the 12 items and agree on a new set of ranks. Your objective is to work towards a team solution that all members of your group can live with and are willing to support. Record your ranks in the column labeled Step two. Once your teamwork begins, do not change your individual ranks.

Ranking the salvaged items

Salvaged items	Step one Individual rank	Step two Team rank	Step three Experts' rank	Step four Difference between 1 & 3	Step five Difference between 2 & 3
Water purification pills					
Bottle of Sedatives					
Pocket compass					
Pocket knife					
Battery operated cassette player with music tapes					
Flashlight					
Insect repellant					
.22 rifle loaded (single shot) with 50 rounds of ammunition					
2 Liter bottles of Johnny Walker Red Label Whisky					
Panga (machete)					
Disposable lighter					
Snake bite kit					
TOTALS (only for steps 4 & 5)					

Experts' ranking

The experts include a game scout, the manager of a safari company and three other 'old Africa hands' (Graham Mercer, Kevin Bartlett, and Nick

Bowley). The combined knowledge of this team equals over 100 years of outdoor expertise in the African bush.

You are approximately 45 kilometers off the tarmac road in a remote part of the Game Park. It is 5.30pm and you have about one-and-a-half hours of daylight left.

It is unlikely that your absence will be noticed at the Tented Camp until the following day. In addition, most of the Park Rangers are away on training and have taken the park vehicles with them. If you wait to be rescued, it could be four or five days. Given that the track you have taken doesn't appear on the visitor's map of the park it could be even longer. Accordingly, you need to take matters into your own hands and walk out.

However, even walking at a brisk clip the tarmac is about 15-18 hours away. If you start immediately, most of the hike will be in the dark. This is risky. You would be wise to remain at the site of the accident overnight and start your walk to the tarmac at first light.

It is very unlikely that you will be attacked by animals unless you surprise them or if they are with their young and feel threatened.

The rule of three states that you can live without oxygen for three minutes, without water for three days, and without food for three weeks. There is no threat to your oxygen. But you do need to be concerned about dehydration. The African sun can be merciless and a 15-18 hour hike without water could be life-threatening. Fortunately at the foot of the valley by the crash site is a small stream.

The other great danger you face is that one or more of your team will be overcome by stress and/or hysteria, which can manifest themselves in many ways. Do not under-estimate the importance of items that can be psychologically comforting.

Item #1: Bottles of Johnny Walker Red Label whisky
This is not party time and it would be unwise to tipple Scotch whisky at this point in your adventure. Not only would the alcohol dull your thinking, it would increase the likelihood of dehydration. However, you do need the bottles to carry water from the stream to your campsite. You might be able to survive without water for 24 hours, but you will be very, very thirsty. Remember, even in the late afternoon the tropical sun is merciless. If the Johnny Walker bottles were not available, you could use

the windscreen washer bottle from the crashed Land Rover.

Item #2: Water purification pills

The water from the stream is probably uncontaminated. The great British explorers Burton and Speke made a journey through this same area, following the old slave route into the interior in 1857. They regularly drank from local streams. However, there is no point in taking chances. These pills will provide you with a safe source of drinking water. Dehydration is your greatest threat.

Item #3: Disposable lighter

This will give you a reliable source of flame. Contrary to popular legend, fire will not scare away big game. However, it will let them know you are in the vicinity. And it is cheering and comforting.

Item #4: Panga

You will need wood to keep the fire going through the night. You will burn the dead branches close to the accident site quickly. You will soon need to cut more wood, particularly larger logs that will burn longer. Splitting logs would be impossible without this tool. And Graham Mercer wrote: 'If you're going to be eaten, you might as well go down fighting.'

Item #5 Flashlight

Not essential, but helpful as you set up your camp and collect wood for the fire. Would also have a beneficial psychological effect.

Item #6: Battery-operated cassette player with music tapes

This will be useful as you walk out in the morning. It will let animals know that you are coming so that you don't surprise them. Alternatively you could sing, but a 14-hour chorus is a stretch and you don't know the quality of your teammates' voices.

Item #7: Pocket knife

It always seems reassuring to have a knife in a survival situation, but the panga is a better tool. The knife would make fire building a little simpler. It is easier to make tinder shavings with a knife than a panga, but if you didn't have it, you wouldn't miss it much.

Item #8: Insect repellant

Probably won't contribute to your survival, but may make the walk back through tsetse fly territory more comfortable. Having said that, tsetses are a very robust species and are immune to most repellants.

Item #9: .22 rifle, loaded

If you had any small game hunting to do, the rifle could be useful. However, it is far too small a caliber to protect you against the most dangerous animals such as lion, buffalo or leopard. It would be like carrying a peashooter. The fact that it is a single-shot is also a huge disadvantage. The great safari guide, Bartle Bull, was fond of saying that it was almost inevitably the second bullet that saved the hunter's life. A wounded animal is much more likely to attack. In terms of using the gun shot noise to ward off animals, the cassette player is a much better device.

Item #10: Snake bite kit

With the exception of black mambas, snakes will generally not attack unless provoked.

A very experienced safari guide wrote that, 'it's almost impossible to be bitten by a snake unless you actually handle snakes, and even then it's unlikely. Green mambas exist in the Mikumi woodlands but are very much arboreal and quite harmless unless you do something really stupid.

'Black mambas can be aggressive but are diurnal and (unless you pose a threat, will get out of your way). Puff adders and other adders are the biggest danger, as they are sluggish and nocturnal and highly venomous. They also like to lie alongside or even on tracks.

'However, the chances of encountering one in these circumstances are extremely rare – they wouldn't approach you at night and in any case you have the flashlight to scour the immediate area, and if any were around on the track the next morning you would see them. So, a very low level threat indeed.'

Item #11: Compass

You know the way to the tarmac. Just follow the track. You don't need the compass unless you do something silly like take a short cut through the woodlands.

Item #12: Bottle of sedatives

As tempting as it might be to take one or two sedatives to calm down after the accident, it is not in your best interest. In any crisis situation, you need to be as mentally sharp as possible. Your life may be dependent on the quality of the decisions you make. Anything that hinders your reasoning, even slightly, could be fatal.

Group scoring

Table Groups	1	2	3	4	5	6	7	8	9	10
Step 6 Average Individual Score										
Step 7 Group Score from Step 5										
Step 8 Gain/Loss in points –subtract Step 7 from Step 6										
Step 9 Percent of gain or loss										
Step 10 Lowest individual score										
Step 11 Number of individual scores lower than the team score										

Case studies in OIQ

The Headmaster shoots himself in the foot
(a case study in self-induced incompetence)

There are few schools anywhere in the world as busy as The Millenium High School. And it would probably be fair to say that there are few women in the world at this moment as angry as Rachel Mauser!

Rachel thrust the keyboard of her computer away from her, clamped her teeth together and seethed. She couldn't believe the email she had received from the Headmaster. Rachel was not prone to strong or vulgar language, but on this occasion…

Rachel was the athletics and activities director at one of the largest and most prestigious private high schools on the Eastern seaboard. It had been her first year in the position and she had worked incredibly hard to make it a success. And by all accounts it had been! Just look at the school calendar on the wall!

Rachel swiveled in her chair. The calendar looked like a diagram of a

First World War battle. Black, blue and red ink competed with yellow highlighter. There wasn't a day that didn't have three or four competing events: sports practices; tournaments; drama rehearsals; music concerts; dance recitals; Model United Nations; forensics competitions; Habitat for Humanity; and a slew of other clubs and community service activities.

Rachel had tried to attend as many as possible. During the last semester she had been out four or five nights a week attending student events. And she had worked the last five weekends – organizing the interschool tennis tournament, the five-a-side football competition, the Spring Carnival, and chaperoning a field trip to the mountains south of the city.

Rachel thought about the Headmaster's email and closed her eyes. Her anger now made her nauseous. Would she have to change all her vacation plans? How would her husband react? Was it worth getting this upset over a job?

The Headmaster's email had reminded Rachel that because she was on a special contract, she was required to work 200 days during the course of an academic year. Pre-empting her questions, the Headmaster went on to say that she could not count evenings or weekends in her annual total and that he did not expect Rachel to start her vacation until ten days after the end of the school year. Needless to say, in her hectic, busy life, Rachel had forgotten this clause in her contract and now, a week before the end of school, it caught her entirely by surprise.

Rachel reached for the phone and dialed the Headmaster's number…

Discussion questions

What conflicting beliefs and values reside at the heart of this problem?

What might be the perceptions that Rachel and the Headmaster each hold about their own identities?

In what ways might this case study represent 'Designed-in' collective stupidity?

Chapter 2

Developing an OIQ focus – teacher leadership for learning

In the Preface we made the claim that if schools are to be transformed and transformative, teachers will lead the way (we would include Principals who see themselves as leaders of adult learning). Let's see how this actually works.

Raising organizational intelligence on the third floor

Janet, Judith and Lynn knew that writing was more than just another means of communication. They understood that it was also way of thinking. Writing provided students with an avenue into deep and complex thought, a means of editing ideas for precision and clarity, and an opportunity to make meaningful connections. For this reason, they and other members of the high school English department at the International School of Kuala Lumpur (ISKL) placed writing at the heart of their curriculum and instruction.

Almost daily the conversation on the third floor (the location of the English department) turned to writing. They discussed different types of writing and how best to introduce them in the classroom: editing techniques; self-assessment; the use of rubrics; organizing principles; and the benefits of publication.

They also asked probing questions: could a teacher who was a poor writer teach writing effectively? What should be the place of creative writing? Do we teach writing or merely evaluate it? Shouldn't all teachers in schools be teachers of writing? They also shared effective instructional strategies for the teaching of writing. At a certain point, a member of the English department suggested that these conversations were so rich that they were worth preserving. And so *The Third Floor* was born.

The Third Floor is a publication of the ISKL high school English department. It includes a mission statement about the value of writing, descriptions of different types of writing and numerous research-based and field-tested strategies for encouraging student writing. Writing *The Third Floor* took over a year and involved every member of the English department. For over a decade, it served as a blueprint for high quality writing instruction.

But the influence of *The Third Floor* was much broader than just a single publication. Janet, Judith and Lynn firmly believed that every teacher at ISKL should be a teacher of writing. They approached the then Headmaster, Dick Krajczar, with the idea that every teacher at ISKL, without exception, should have to take a process-writing course. Not only did Dick agree to the proposal; he had it written into all new teacher contracts. This is doubly remarkable because Dick (as he will be the first to admit) has always struggled with writing himself! In fact, Dick was among the first to sign up for the now mandatory writing course.

The influence of *The Third Floor* didn't end at the ISKL perimeter fence. Out of the rich discussions about writing came the idea for an East Asia Writing Project which, for more than ten years, has offered summer workshops for teachers in Malaysia, Singapore, India, the Philippines and Hong Kong.

Janet, Judith and Lynn and their colleagues in the ISKL English department cultivated a pocket of high organizational intelligence. They came together around a compelling vision (developing the writing skills of all students), nurtured collective efficacy and supported each other in their efforts to build leadership capacity. They systematically broadened their sphere of responsibility from their individual classrooms, to their department, to the entire school, and finally extended it to include all international schools in East Asia. This was a moment in time when teachers reclaimed our profession.

In search of a metaphor

Several years ago we were researching an article on school organizational intelligence and seeking a metaphor that would capture our thoughts on this complex subject. At the same time we came upon the European sheep dog trials.

If you have never seen sheep dog trials, a brief word of introduction is in order. These are timed competitions which pit shepherds and their incredibly well-trained dogs against each other to measure the speed and efficiency with which they can move and organize a flock of sheep. The trials begin with a shepherd standing on a wooden platform at one end of a huge field, which is surrounded by spectators.

In the field a hundred or so sheep are scattered; sheep that neither shepherd nor dog has seen before. The shepherd gives a series of commands to his Border collie, which proceeds to round up the flock and herd it to a relatively small circle marked on the grass at the other end of the field.

Once the sheep are within the circle, the shepherd calls out another specific instruction: the collie then locates one sheep that has been distinctively marked, separates it from the flock while keeping the rest within the circle, and brings it to his master. To say we were impressed would be an understatement.

During this same time, we read a great deal about school leadership competencies. Everyone and his uncle seemed to have drafted a checklist of basic competencies and skills that the school leader needed. We were troubled by the narrow and behaviorist approach to the concept of school leadership.

We wondered whether dynamic leadership could really be achieved simply via a laundry list of behavioral competencies? Was school leadership simply the acquisition of a toolbox of skills – a paint by number mix and match of situations and appropriate responses? We asked each other what characteristics truly effective teacher leaders shared. And amid these musings ran flocks of sheep, skillfully chased by Border collies.

Finally, a troubling question came into our thinking. If educational leadership could be reduced to a checklist of behaviors, a hefty toolbox of strategies, was it not analogous to the movement of sheep from one end of a field to another?

We found the question troubling because at least some of the research we had been reading had tacitly adopted such a model. The more we thought about it, the more distressing the question became. A Principal assigns children and teachers to classes, organizes a master schedule of classes, arranges for the inventory of teaching supplies and sets attainable curricular targets.

Within the classroom, the teacher groups children into cooperative learning teams, sets behavioral expectations and then takes her students through the stages of expanding literacy and numeracy. These are necessary tasks of school organization and class management, and there is nothing inherently wrong with management and organization. Why was the shepherd analogy troubling? Going all the way back to Biblical times, the conscientious shepherd has a long and noble history as a diligent and caring figure.

But the metaphor is hollow because it doesn't address the purpose of teacher leadership. Drawing on the work of Linda Lambert (1998), Richard Elmore (2000), James Spillane (Spillane & Sherer, 2004; Spillane, Halverson, & Diamond, 2004) and others we would like to suggest that the ultimate purpose of school leadership, whether it is practiced by Principals, team leaders or teachers, is to develop and enhance organizational intelligence by *developing leadership capacity in others* – our colleagues and our students. It is building leadership capacity in others that transforms the hearts and minds of all who inhabit the schoolhouse.

When sheep are moved from one field to another, they remain intrinsically unchanged. In some schools the same might be true for students and teachers. As young people are taken in an orderly and efficient fashion from the meadows of ancient civilizations to the fields of the Renaissance, from the pastures of Dickens and the Brontë sisters to the plains of Hemingway and Fitzgerald, they too may remain unchanged.

The fields may change, but like skillfully herded sheep, the students remain largely unaltered by the experience. This is a travesty of education. Unconnected and irrelevant information has been poured into young vessels, but the vessel itself is in much the same shape as it was before the so-called learning experience.

A similar analogy can be made for teachers. We attend conferences and workshops and learn a few new strategies. This is *informational learning,* much like moving sheep from one field to another. The teacher remains largely unchanged by the experience. Piaget (1957) called this learning by assimilation whereby the individual takes in new information without changing his or her fundamental way of thinking or acting. Contrast Piaget's concept of learning by accommodation where the individual makes internal changes to him or herself in order to fit a changing world or changing perceptions of the world.

In order to develop enhanced organizational intelligence, teachers and school leaders need to engage in *transformational* learning and this is when we strive to build leadership capacity in others. School people are actually changed by transformational learning. Our hearts and minds are affected. We are not the same creatures that once grazed on the other side of the fence. When we build leadership capacity in others we create the school climate where learning relationships can flourish. This is enhanced OIQ.

Redefining school leadership

When we write about school leadership, we are referring to the professionals in the schoolhouse who have been charged with the design and implementation of learning: teachers are by definition leaders of learning. They lead the learning of their students. They also lead their own learning. And in schools with high organizational intelligence, they also lead the learning of their colleagues.

Each summer Bill teaches a course on leadership and group dynamics at The Principal's Training Center attended by principals, team leaders and teachers. At the start of the course Bill asks the table groups to come to consensus on what is the most important purpose of school leadership.

Inevitably a large number of groups come up with something along the lines of 'improving student learning'. The problems with this response are that it is both true and false and, most of all, a platitude that is rarely examined.

The truth is that principals are rarely in a position to *directly* influence student learning. This is the teacher's role. Principals and school leaders often do little or no direct teaching of students. However, principals can have a powerful indirect influence on students learning by leading *adult* learning. It is curious to note that the leading of adult *transformative* learning has received little attention in graduate level school leadership or administrative certification programs.

In order for educators to raise the collective intelligence of their schools, they must lead adult, transformative learning. They do so by engaging in two parallel processes. The first we refer to as the 'Data to Wisdom Continuum' and the second as 'Embedded Learning'. When these processes are simultaneously brought into schools, faculty come to understand the mission and vision of the organization both as individuals and as a collective. They see their part in moving the school forward and accept their responsibility in improving student learning. The OIQ factor of the school has been enhanced.

Transformational learning involves a progression on the Data to Wisdom Continuum, which involves the following stages:

Data
Information
Knowledge
Wisdom

Data
Data represent the raw results of our inquiry. Data are factually accurate notes, observations or statistics, but are meaningless in and of themselves. If we conducted a classroom assessment and 60% of the students failed, this would be data. No analysis has been undertaken; the raw results provide no meaning. At the data stage, we have no clue as to why 60% of the students have failed.

Information
The next step on the data to knowledge continuum is the arrangement of data into information. Here we see the beginning of pattern making. We look for categories or similarities. When we arrange data into information, we may find superficial meaning or we may reach hastily arrived-at conclusions, but we achieve no deep understanding.

If we go back to our example of an assessment that 60% of the students failed, we might say that the majority didn't understand the concept or could not demonstrate the requisite skills. We might also jump to the conclusion that either the content was developmentally inappropriate or that they were poorly taught; or perhaps that the majority of the class was lazy and didn't study. At this stage there is no support for our conclusions. Unfortunately, sometimes inquiries in schools end at the information stage and very poor decisions are taken as a result.

Knowledge

From information we can move to the knowledge stage. In order to create knowledge we need to engage in rigorous cognitive processes such as analysis, synthesis and evaluation. We need to make tentative connections, evaluate them, and then frame and test hypotheses. This is hard cognitive labor, which benefits exponentially from collaborative effort.

In our example where 60% of the class failed an assessment, we might start the knowledge-making process by doing an item analysis of the assessment itself. Were there common questions that many of the students missed? If so, did these items have shared characteristics? Was the problem with the assessment itself? Were the questions poorly or ambiguously worded? Were there terms that might have been foreign to some of the students? Was there cultural bias (*eg* asking predominantly Indonesian students how many nickels in a dollar)? Was there a common concept or process that the students may not have understood?

Next, we might look at the learning profile of students who missed the same questions. Were they second language English speakers? From our analysis, we can frame questions and then test the questions. If the process is rigorous, meaningful knowledge can emerge.

Up to this point, we have engaged in primarily *informational* learning.

Wisdom

But knowledge, however meaningful, is not the same as wisdom. Wisdom is higher order knowledge that goes beyond the available meaning in order to arrive at new insights based upon our learning and experience. Wisdom is where *transformational* learning takes place, because wisdom changes who we are, what we believe and value, how we behave and in some cases how we actually make sense and meaning of the world around us. Pfeffer and Sutton (2006 p174) capture the essence of this in their definition of wisdom: 'Wisdom is the ability to act with knowledge while doubting what you know.'

Continuing with our example of the class where 60% of the students failed an assessment, the analysis might have revealed that the majority of students missed questions that focused on a single concept, let's say 'entropy', in high school physics. Since the wording of the questions was clear, we must assume that the failure was a lack of understanding on the part of the students. As their teacher, I had failed to create the conditions under which deep and transferable understanding would occur.

I remember feeling a little pressured while I was teaching about entropy. I felt a bit rushed. There was a lot of content to be covered. Had I taught 'entropy' too quickly? (Here is the knowledge hypothesis.) How do I go about planning the pacing of my lessons (here is the question that leads from knowledge to wisdom)? Do I pace lessons based on the needs of my teaching or the needs of student learning? If pacing should be related to student learning, how can I learn about their learning? How am I redefining my relationship with my students? How am I redefining my sense of professional identity?

We refer to the second process involved in transformative learning as Embedded Learning. The anthropologist Gregory Bateson (in Garmston, 2005) first suggested the idea of relating systems of learning to human growth. Later both Robert Kegan (1994, 2009) and Robert Dilts (1994) developed this idea further. Dilts identified four levels of nested or embedded learning: identity; beliefs and values; capabilities; and behaviors that form a hierarchy of learning outcomes.

Levels of Embedded Learning
Identity
Values and Beliefs
Capabilities
Behaviors

Behaviors
Starting with the last on the list, teachers learning at the level of behaviors might include mastering instructional strategies that serve to improve students' learning. Examples might be learning to use a 'jigsaw' strategy or providing students with 3 to 5 seconds of wait time after the teacher has asked a question. Instructional strategies are important, but when they are taught in isolation they are learned as information fragments and represent episodic learning that have a remarkably short life span in our procedural memory.

Learning objectives at the behavior level are at the bottom of Anderson's Taxonomy (2001). They involve low-level informational learning, which is rarely transferred effectively and sustainably to the classroom. Learning at the level of behavior doesn't provide for meaningful self-assessment.

Capabilities

Capabilities are clusters of behaviors that serve a common purpose, mental maps used to guide behaviors. Learning at the level of capabilities involves making connections between behaviors and understanding how they may be related to each other. It also involves understanding the bigger picture and allows for self-assessment. 'To elegantly perform an activity or behavior requires learning at the level of Capabilities.' (Garmston, 2005, p15).

An example of a learning objective at the level of capabilities might be for teachers to enhance their instructional strategies in order to evoke deep critical and creative thinking on the part of their students. To this end, we might introduce teachers to the concept of wait time and have them generate reflective questions that involve cognition at the upper end of Anderson's Taxonomy.

Learning at the level of capabilities allows for meaningful self-assessment – the difference between: am I using wait time regularly (behavioral level); or have I seen an improvement in student thinking (capabilities level)? An even more reflective question might be: what connections am I observing between my use of wait time and student thinking?

Learning objectives at the level of behaviors and capabilities involve *informational* learning. *Transformational* learning happens when the learning objectives are designed at the level of beliefs/values and identity. It is learning at these levels that provides the opportunity to enhance organizational intelligence.

Values and beliefs

Values and beliefs are *assumptions* we hold to be true about the way things work: what is important; what is worthy; and about what may be good or evil. Assumptions have a very powerful influence on our behavior and decision-making. They include our guidelines for moral and ethical behavior, what constitutes a healthy relationship, and how each of us might balance our needs with those of other people.

While some values and beliefs are held consciously many, perhaps even most, of our assumptions are held at sub-conscious levels. Values and beliefs often express themselves in our decision-making. For example, a teacher who believes that intelligence is fixed by heredity (a belief at either conscious or sub-conscious levels) may be more liable to give up on a struggling child than one who believes that intelligence is to some degree malleable depending on appropriate supports and challenges.

When we bring our assumptions to the surface, analyze them and explore their implications, we are engaged in transformational learning.

Identity

Learning at the level of identity is the essence of transformation. It literally alters who we believe we are. While it is tempting to think of this kind of learning as those once-in-a-lifetime blinding flashes of insight (such as St. Paul's conversion [Saul of Tarsus] on the road to Damascus), learning at the level of identity is not as uncommon as it may seem.

When we engage with content that conflicts with previous knowledge, we explore the possibility of a change in who we are. Whenever we enter a new role (teacher, principal, staff developer) we shift our perception as to our identity. Whenever we have a flash of insight or make a new connection, the potential is there for an alteration in who we perceive ourselves to be. Teachers and school leaders need to be at the forefront of the examination of professional identity. This should be the stated purpose behind all adult professional learning – the discovery of who we are and the vision of who we wish to become.

Education is a field in which there is an enormous amount of uncertainty. There is vastly more that we don't know about teaching and learning than what presently comprises our professional frame of reference. Thus it stands to reason that we should approach our sense of professional identity as a dynamic process of on-going revelation.

Regular and rigorous participation in these two processes – data to wisdom continuum and embedded learning – bring a degree of clarity and transparency to the teaching process and enhances the overall OIQ factor in our schools.

The myth of the status quo

So why is it so important for teachers and school leaders to design their work so that it enhances organizational intelligence?

The simple answer is that there is no status quo in schools. School people who see their jobs as maintenance are deluding themselves. Schools, like any other organization, are either improving or deteriorating. And schools do not improve by default or benign neglect. They improve by design.

We have seen many school reform initiatives that have failed or are failing because the focus has been on accountability as opposed to responsibility. Accountability is imposed and is external to self. We hold other people accountable. The central office holds the principals accountable, principals hold teachers accountable, and teachers do the same to students. It can easily become a vicious circle of blame seeking, mistrust and buck-passing.

When we make accountability our goal, we operate on the assumption that the individual will do as little as he or she can get away with and therefore needs to be held accountable. This often takes the form of coercive rewards and punishments and diminishes personal and collective responsibility. It can actually infantilize people. We hear people say: "Why should I go the extra mile? What's in it for me? Is there a stipend for the extra work?" External rewards and punishments are examples of designed-in stupidity.

Responsibility, on the other hand, is internal to self. It is the driving force behind all professional learning: our desire to improve our craft and to meet the needs of very diverse student and adult learners. Schools with a high degree of organizational intelligence invite teachers to re-examine and broaden their sphere of responsibility and become self-directed as we saw in Janet, Judith and Lynn at ISKL. The underlying message is that responsibility is a shared endeavor. The metaphoric 'No trespassing' signs have been removed.

Shared responsibility grows in tandem with a sense of belonging and membership. When teachers feel that they are part of a meaningful community, they will often demonstrate a sense of responsibility that extends far beyond the door of their classroom.

This may be seen in many simple and concrete actions. When a teacher, assigned to supervision duty on the playground during recess, stoops to pick up a piece of litter, she is demonstrating responsibility that transcends what she is required to perform. When a teacher corrects the corridor behavior of a child from a different class we are seeing an expanding sphere of responsibility. Teacher leaders who enhance organizational intelligence cultivate professional responsibility in their colleagues.

Teacher leadership:
the intersection of the professional and the personal

In many schools, professional learning is viewed as either an individual or institutional activity. In other words, the goals serve either the individual or the institution. Teachers are asked to write individual professional development goals at the start of a school year or the school leadership team determines school wide institutional goals.

A teacher may be focused on goals that will enhance personal career objectives. The principal may be concerned with goals to support student achievement in specific curriculum areas. Either way, the goals may not be developed collectively. To be transformative, setting professional learning goals needs to be a collective endeavor with teachers and administrators learning together, planning together, coaching and reflecting together.

The development of teacher leadership involves knowledge, skills and dispositions. Our values and beliefs, the cornerstone of our professional identity, are most often displayed in our dispositions. In which situations do we choose to demonstrate courage, compassion, trust, resolve or perseverance? When we cultivate leadership in self and others there is no separation between the professional and personal.

When the school leadership is absent from a professional learning opportunity such as a workshop, teachers often get the message that this is a 'teacher activity' and that the important people in the school have better and more important things to do. This lowers the organizational intelligence of the school. Superintendents, directors, and principals who do not see themselves first and foremost as educators and learners should find another profession.

Making organizational intelligence visible

One very powerful way that school leaders can enhance the OIQ factor is by giving teachers permission to learn. They do this by publicly modeling learning themselves. They read educational publications and talk about their reading, attend workshops, conferences and courses. When there is a professional development opportunity at their school, they attend. They share articles on teaching and learning and participate in discussion and study groups.

Teacher leaders who deliberately raise the OIQ factor use the language of thinking. They talk publicly about cognitive processes such as analysis, synthesis and evaluation. They ask questions that they don't know the answers to. They suspend judgment and wonder out loud. They speculate and then publicly change their mind when the evidence doesn't support their initial position. They engage in meta-cognition, asking, for example, how does this knowledge complement or conflict with my prior knowledge?

Teachers and school leaders who engage in transformational learning model thoughtfulness. They have the self-confidence to display uncertainty publically. They appreciate complexity and ambiguity. They may also employ thinking routines such as: 'What's going on here/What makes you say so?' or 'I used to think.../Now I think...' (Ritchart *et al* 2011).

Educators who enhance organizational intelligence have growth mindsets (Dweck 2008) in that they perceive a causal relationship between effort and achievement for themselves as well as their schools.

Guided study questions

What are some of your hunches as to what made The Third Floor initiative at ISKL successful? What similar initiatives have you seen at your school? What are you taking away from this analysis that may be useful in the future?

What may be opportunities for you to use the Data-to-Wisdom Continuum at your own school? Have you noticed premature closure to some professional conversations? What might be some facilitation strategies that would allow knowledge and wisdom to emerge?

When planning adult learning opportunities, what are some ways to take into account the Levels of Embedded Learning?

In what ways are teacher leaders making organizational intelligence visible in your school?

Card stack and shuffle activity

Directions for facilitator: Tell participants that each of us holds a variety of assumptions about teaching and learning that exert a powerful influence over our classroom instructional behavior and decision-making. Many of these assumptions are held at sub-conscious levels that are not explicitly examined. This activity affords us an opportunity to surface and analyze our assumptions and to identify their implications.

Participants sit in groups of five or six. Each participant is given two index cards, upon which they complete two sentence stems which can be on any subject worthy of reflective inquiry. For example, if we wanted to examine our assumptions about collective intelligence, the sentence stems might be:

Evidence of high collective intelligence...

I contribute to enhanced group intelligence...

One member of the group collects the cards and shuffles them. The cards are then passed to another table so that no table group analyzes its own assumptions. Table groups spend approximately 30 to 40 minutes analyzing the sentences, the assumptions that lie beneath them and the implications. There is then a large group debrief that might focus on the interesting patterns that have emerged from analyses.

Case studies in OIQ

Case study one: 'You can't do that in the high school'

Devon Turnbull recognized that he was feeling irritable. Why was the pushback always coming from the high school? Devon had been the director of the International School of the North Sea for the past eight years and had led the school-wide initiative to personalize student learning.

Devon felt strongly that students should be provided with differentiated opportunities to access the curriculum. Both the elementary and middle schools had made good progress, but the high school seemed stuck in a rut. Devon wasn't sure what the problem was. His background was in primary school leadership and the high school had always been a bit of a mystery.

Over the past three years, the International School of the North Sea had framed its annual goals around differentiated instruction and personalized learning. It had purchased resources, formed study groups, brought in external consultants and had experts model what differentiation might look like. The administration had used the Looking for Learning protocol to examine how personalized learning was being integrated into the classrooms. The school had even set up a 'personalized learning blog' to which teachers could post questions and comments. The process was going fairly well in the elementary school and the middle school, but not so in the high school.

"What, specifically, are issues that the high school teachers are facing?" Devon asked Brian Mondial, the high school principal.

Brian paused. They had been through this before. "There isn't time for personalized learning. The content demands of programs like the IB and AP don't leave time for differentiation. Anyway, the teachers say that neither IB nor AP assessments are differentiated, so they don't see the relevance. It just doesn't work in the high school."

Devon Turnbull didn't buy it. A year later an opportunity presented itself. Brian Mondial announced that he would be leaving the International School of the North Sea to pursue an advanced degree in education. Devon contemplated launching a search for Brian's replacement, but ultimately decided that he would not.

He decided instead that, for one year, he would assume not only the directorship of the school but also the responsibilities of the high school principal. His objective was to determine whether personalized learning really didn't work in the high school.

He called a meeting of high school teachers and announced his decision to serve as interim high school principal for the next school year. He explained that his background was primarily in elementary school and that this would be a learning experience for him. He went on to say that he was interested in exploring with the high school teachers what was and wasn't possible in terms of instructional pedagogy and how teachers might balance the demands of the curriculum with student learning needs.

His announcement was greeted with mixed reactions. A few teachers welcomed it and felt that the high school could greatly benefit from such an intervention. A few teachers were openly hostile and mistrustful. Many were confused and uncertain.

But Devon was true to his word and engaged in inquiry-based leadership. He didn't shy away from difficult issues or teachers who were only marginally effective, but he approached them with data and questions, not judgments. In his own words, he provided 'relentless support'. By the end of the year, three high school teachers had decided that the direction the school was going in was not for them and announced their intention to move on to other schools. Devon respected their decisions. The remainder were, for the most part, on board with personalized learning and a number had significantly enhanced student learning in their classrooms.

Discussion questions

In what ways has Devon demonstrated inquiry-based leadership?

How has Devon moved the high school towards the goals of a professional learning community?

Chapter 3

Emotional intelligence and the OIQ factor

Emotional intelligence has been studied for many years, but came to prominence in 1985 when Daniel Goleman published a book by the same title. Goleman has gone on to research the many connections between emotional intelligence and effective leadership. In 2010, Bill and Ochan published a book entitled *Becoming an Emotionally Intelligent Teacher*.

There are two premises in the book. The first is that emotionally intelligent teachers are better equipped to develop classroom relationships that support student learning. This is crucial because most meaningful (transformative) learning takes place in a social setting (Vygotsky, 1986) – within relationships. The second is that emotional intelligence can be learned and developed.

In this chapter, we will take the idea of emotional intelligence a step further. We will examine how emotional intelligence permeates virtually every aspect of our individual and collective lives in schools. Secondly, we will look specifically at the role of emotional intelligence in developing classrooms with high organizational intelligence. We will examine the process of building leadership capacity in students and colleagues and how this may be related to the process of school re-culturing.

But let's begin our exploration of emotional intelligence with a story.

Brigadier General Dozier's bad day

December 17th, 1981, was probably one of the worst days in the life of US Brigadier General James Dozier, for whom it was filled with fear and anger. It was the day that he was kidnapped. General Dozier was serving as Deputy Chief of Staff at NATO's Southern European Headquarters and was the highest ranking US military officer in Italy.

At approximately 6pm Dozier answered the front door bell of his apartment in Verona, Italy. Four men dressed as plumbers, carrying bags of tools burst in, took firearms from the bags and held Dozier at gunpoint. Although the General was armed he did not attempt to use his weapon – perhaps out of concern for the safety of his wife, who was also at home.

The kidnappers were members of a cell of the Red Brigades, an ultra-left wing terrorist organization that was attempting to topple the Italian government. They bound Dozier and placed him in a truck. They did not kidnap Mrs Dozier, who was left gagged and chained in the apartment.

Brigadier General James Dozier was held by the Red Brigade terrorists for 42 days, often bound and chained with loud heavy metal music pumped through headphones.

News of his abduction caused a feeding frenzy among the media of both Europe and the United States that had a predictable effect on his kidnappers. They became excitable, irrational and anxious. Each new newspaper clipping and breaking news television report made them more unstable.

Dozier recognized that the more agitated and irrational his kidnappers became, the more likely they were to execute him. Then he recalled something he had learned from an executive development program at the Center for Creative Leadership: emotions are contagious.

Dozier realized two critical features of his captive situation. First, he must not 'catch' the panic and excitement of his guards. Secondly, he must try to 'infect' them with emotional stability by modeling his own calmness.

Years later, Dozier reflected on how his learning about emotional intelligence had helped to save his life:

> The most important thing that I took away from the Center's program was to learn how to see myself through the eyes of others... That led me to two intuitive things that enhanced my chances of survival.

First, in order to forestall violent reactions on the part of the guards, I tried to make myself a more reliable prisoner by conducting myself as they would expect a general to so do. I did so by establishing a set daily routine and behaving accordingly. Secondly, by repeatedly asking questions about my wife, I attempted to get them to see me as a human being, rather than just a prisoner.

His strategy worked. The General's kidnappers became calmer and less vigilant. They began bringing him newspaper clippings to show that his wife and family were fine. On 28th January, 1982, after six weeks in captivity, an Italian national level counter-terrorism team rescued the General from an apartment in Padua.

General Dozier's experience illustrates dramatically how a single individual's emotionally intelligent leadership can affect the thinking of others and arguably raise the collective intelligence (or at least diminish the irrational volatility) of even a very hostile group.

Like General Dozier, teacher leaders who effectively support their organizations in managing change need first to be aware of and to manage their own feelings of anxiety and uncertainty (Cherniss & Goleman, 2001).

EQ is the cornerstone of OIQ

We would argue that enhanced organizational intelligence goes hand-in-hand with increased collective emotional intelligence. No school improvement initiative, no matter how well thought through, how well planned, how well communicated and justified, stands any chance of success unless it also improves relationships within the schoolhouse (Barth, 1990; Barth, 2006; Fullan 2000).

Learning in schools takes place for the most part within relationships – relationships between teachers and students, between teachers and teachers, and between teachers and principals. The quality of those relationships often determines the depth of the learning that takes place. Relationships that are based upon respect and trust are much more likely to foster and promote transformational learning than those based on coercion and fear.

Emotional intelligence is the cornerstone to building healthy learning relationships and therefore promoting organizational intelligence. This is supported by research (Woolley, Chabris, Pentland, Hashmi & Malone,

2010) that found a significant correlation between enhanced collective intelligence of groups and the social sensitivity of the group members. Fullan suggests (2001) that effective teacher leaders work on their own and others' emotional development. 'There is no greater skill needed for sustainable (school) improvement' (p74).

Individual and collective emotional intelligence influences our work in schools in a number of areas:

Professional development of teachers;
employee recruitment and retention;
collaboration and teamwork;
Innovation and openness to change;
productivity and efficiency;
quality of relationships – teacher/student, teacher/admin, teacher/parent;
and, most importantly, student learning.

The three Ps of emotional intelligence

In the previous chapter, we suggested that teachers engage in enhancing organizational intelligence when they promote transformational learning in themselves and other adults in their schools. This is the essence of school re-culturing. This transformational learning often takes place when we deliberately strive to build leadership capacity in others.

In many schools the development of leadership capacity happens by default. We do not consciously set out to develop it. We simply provide opportunities for teachers or students to take on additional responsibilities and then we evaluate how well they have performed. We often throw them in the deep end; they either sink or swim; and we talk about 'leadership potential' as though it were an inherited trait, not something that can and should be developed.

An uncomfortable truth that most educators have to face at some point in their careers is that no one can compel learning in another person. This is hard for many teachers and parents to accept, but is true nevertheless. The decision to learn is an internal one that can be influenced by previous experience, readiness, our perceived sense of competence, our emotional state, our interests, and self-confidence. Teachers can set the conditions for learning, but the actual decision to learn is always made by the learner. For this reason, the most effective teachers develop leadership capacity in students and colleagues through mediation and ongoing coaching.

Mediation is the process of supporting the thinking and learning of a student or valued colleague (Costa & Garmston, 2002) and is accomplished by using the three Ps of emotional intelligence: *pausing, paraphrasing* and *probing.* These are three powerful other-centered strategies that support growth, often transformational growth, in other people. When teachers regularly use the strategies of pausing, paraphrasing and probing in their classrooms, we see deep student inquiry; when adults regularly employ the three Ps of EQ in professional conversations we see enhanced collective intelligence.

When these three strategies are linked to what Costa and Garmston (2002) refer to as the Five States of Mind, we have the potential for building leadership capacity in others. But, before we get to the States of Mind, let's pause and examine these three P's of emotional intelligence in more depth. In other words, let's pause for a pause.

Pausing: slowing down the frames per second

Pausing slows down the number of frames per second of a conversation. It sends the message that, in this conversation, thinking is not only permissible but also welcome. We don't need to have arrived at the conversation with ready-made and well-rehearsed ideas. It is acceptable to have new insights and to change our mind. Pausing in our adult-to-adult conversations draws on the same research that supports Mary Budd Rowe's contention that teacher use of wait time in the classroom dramatically enhances student critical and creative thinking. We need to respect the silence.

In the West there is often the misperception that the speed with which we respond somehow equates to intelligence. In other words, the faster one can think on one's feet, the more intelligent the individual. Curiously this does not tend to be the perception in the East. In Asia intelligence is often characterized by the time taken to ponder over something. Pausing also signals that what we have heard is worthy of deep consideration and as such is highly respectful.

Pausing gives us access to our menu of response behaviors and can thus help us to avoid impulsiveness. We can choose whether to frown, laugh, make a judgment or ask a question. Pausing allows us to identify our intentions and then choose congruent behavior.

Pausing also serves as a powerful preventative to personalized conflict. Think back to a destructive personalized conflict that you have witnessed in the past. The chances are that you saw the speed of the interchange escalate. Someone said something and the other person responded and the rapidity of the interaction increased until someone said something that they may have regretted afterwards. Pausing can prevent such personalized conflict and can serve to foster interpersonal trust.

Paraphrasing, not parrot-phrasing

The second P of emotional intelligence, paraphrasing, got a bad name in the 1970s when we thought of it as a linguistic tool and taught each other stems like 'What I think I hear you saying is…' The stem seemed to imply social manipulation and made people feel as though they were being sold a second-hand car.

We now know that paraphrasing isn't a linguistic tool; it is a much under-used listening tool. Paraphrasing is capturing the essence of what someone has said and reflecting it back to the person in one's own words. It is not parrot-phrasing.

Both of us undertake a great deal of paraphrase training when teaching Cognitive Coaching skills (Costa & Garmston, 2002). Most participants are initially surprised at how cognitively demanding and difficult elegant paraphrasing is.

We know that summary writing is a most effective, research-based learning strategy that teachers can use in the classroom (Marzano 2001). It requires students to read a piece of text, separate the peripheral from the central idea(s) and then restate that important idea in their own words. It often involves rigorous analysis, evaluation and synthesis. Paraphrasing is the oral equivalent to summary writing, but can be even more challenging because you don't have the script to reread. High-quality paraphrasing demands intense concentration and focused attention.

Paraphrasing supports the thinking of another person or a group as it engages in inquiry. Paraphrasing can be used to acknowledge and clarify, help organize the thinking of another person, or to support the other person in reaching deeper levels of thought and conceptualization.

Paraphrasing is a most powerful tool of emotional intelligence because it sends three, highly respectful messages:

I am listening to you;
I understand (or I am trying to understand) what you are saying; and,
I care about what you're saying (and, by implication, I care about you).

Some participants in our workshops express concern that a paraphrase might be interpreted by the other person as condescending or patronizing. This is not our experience. If the paraphrase is a genuine attempt to understand the other person, and the tone of voice reflects this sincerity, it is very unlikely to give offense. If it is skillfully crafted the chances are the other person will not even recognize it as a paraphrase. He or she will simply think you are a good and respectful listener.

Probing for clarity or specificity

Probing is the process of asking gentle, invitational questions that serve to support the other person in gaining either greater clarity or specificity. Psychologists tell us that any question, no matter how gently worded, sets up a psychological distance between the person asking and the person receiving the question.

We can mitigate this distance to some extent by using the approachable voice, employing plural forms and exploratory language, embedding positive presuppositions and preceding the probing question with a paraphrase (Costa & Garmston 2002).

It is axiomatic that respectful behavior is the hallmark of high quality conversations, whether between teachers and students in the classroom or between teachers as they plan units or design assessments. Having said that, few conversations actually unpack the specifics of what constitutes respectful behavior. We would assert that the foundation of all respect is genuine and active listening. Without such listening, all other attempts at respectful behavior will be ineffectual. Pausing, paraphrasing and probing are strategies that promote structured inquiry and raise organizational intelligence.

Organizational intelligence: building leadership capacity in others

Enhancing the collective intelligence of a group involves deliberately developing leadership capacity in others. Leadership, in the sense we are using it, isn't necessarily limited to ascribed positions of authority such as principal, team leader, chairperson or coordinator. Leadership can also be thought of as learning to lead oneself, as in self-directedness – the capacity that we develop to self-manage, self-monitor and self-modify.

Costa and Garmston (2002) have identified Five States of Mind that interact to promote both internal and external leadership. When we combine sensitivity to these states of mind with the three Ps of emotional intelligence we can support the growth of leadership capacity in others. These states of mind are internal resources that influence our perceptions and accordingly can enhance or inhibit our responses to life's challenges. 'These basic human forces drive, influence, motivate, and inspire our intellectual capacities, emotional responsiveness, high performance and productive human action (p124).' When these states of mind are in high internal resource, effective self-direction emerges. The states of mind are: efficacy, flexibility, craftsmanship, consciousness and interdependence. Let's look at each in turn.

The five states of mind

Efficacy is the belief that the individual can cope with the present and influence and effect desired change in the future. It is the belief that 'I can make a difference', that my contribution is important, that in some meaningful way I can be the architect of my own future.

Efficacious people are problem solvers; they believe that their behavior can influence outcomes. They see complex dilemmas as opportunities, are optimistic, self-actualizing, cognitively active and lifelong learners. Efficacious people realistically accord responsibility to others and self; they are not simply the passive recipients of other people's decisions.

High efficacy suggests a strong internal locus of control. These are not the blaming voices of withdrawal, manufactured excuses, helplessness, rigidity and resistance to change. Individuals who are governed by an internal locus of control take the initiative in affecting change in their environment, controlling impulsivity, systematically gathering data and showing signs of humor.

From 1979 to 1982, researchers at the University of Chicago attempted to discover why some high pressure, business executives became physically ill from stress and others did not. The executives with low illness were shown to be strong in three areas: commitment, control and challenge. In short, they were highly efficacious individuals (Lefcourt, 1982).

Flexibility is the intellectual and emotional ability and willingness to step out of oneself and look at a specific situation from different perspectives. It involves a willingness to take risks, to entertain new ideas and to discard cherished but fallacious theories.

Flexibility demands that the individual overcome the tyranny of egocentrism and embrace the reality of awe-inspiring 'otherness'. In its nascence, flexibility is as simple and as complex as recognizing that the other person is as complicated, sensitive, intelligent and as emotionally needy as oneself. This is a remarkable discovery that comes to some early, some late and some not at all.

Flexible people practice empathy. They become accustomed to leaving the familiarity of their own shoes and are comfortable with the foreignness of standing in the footwear of others. This practiced empathy allows the individual to predict misunderstandings and accordingly extend to others the benefit of the doubt, the assumption of a positive intention and good faith.

Flexible people recognize the powerful influence of perceptions on thought and behavior and are constantly asking themselves: is there another way to interpret this situation? Flexible people appreciate that perceptions are manufactured and, as such, malleable.

Craftsmanship is the driving force that propels us to improve in whatever work we undertake. The craftsman strives after excellence and precision, taking pride in both the process and the product of her labor. Whether it is the concert pianist, the master teacher, the Olympic athlete or the persevering scholar, craftsmen work to expand their present expertise, to polish their current performance and to improve and enhance the product of hard work. Risking, reflecting and refining are the essence of craftsmanship (Kusuma-Powell & Powell, 2000).

Craftsmanship is an energy source that compels people towards clarity, refinement and precision. The craftsman tirelessly strives to deepen her knowledge and improve her skills, setting goals that are beyond the present level of performance and monitoring the process made towards those goals.

Consciousness is one's awareness of the events surrounding oneself and the understanding of one's own thoughts, feelings and impressions. Consciousness operates at a multitude of levels. At its highest level it involves introspection and the perilous journey into self-knowledge. To be conscious is to know what is going on *both outside and within oneself.*

Individuals who have developed high degrees of consciousness monitor the interface between their thoughts and feelings and the events of the external environment. They reflect and question. They are able to put distance between themselves and their thoughts and so approach their own mental processes with a scrutiny that is normally reserved for others. Highly conscious people explicate clearly-defined value systems that are then employed as criteria for decision making.

Consciousness is not simply awareness; it is self-directed knowledge. It is that state of mind that educational researchers call 'with-it-ness', an individual's ability 'to be aware of and respond to a multitude of social cues, many happening simultaneously, and respond appropriately and constructively'. Teachers with low consciousness may not survive long in the classroom.

Interdependence is developed when the individual links a sense of autonomy to membership in a community. The community can be as small as a monogamous marriage or as large as one of the world's great religions. Interdependent people come to see themselves as individuals who are able and willing to lend their energies to the achievement of group goals. They are able to suspend selfishness and work towards the good of the larger number.

Interdependent individuals are comfortable giving and receiving support. They are sensitive to both their own needs and the needs of others. They know when to integrate and when to assert.

Historically, interdependence has *not* been a hallmark of schools; teachers worked for the most part in isolation from other adults and when students attempted to collaborate (to learn from each other) they were often accused of cheating.

Isolation is the opposite of interdependence and is the enemy of organizational intelligence. As a punishment, isolation (solitary confinement) is reserved for the most recalcitrant criminals. In very young children prolonged physical or emotional isolation can have crippling psychological effects and in some cases can actually be life-threatening.

Individuals with a strong sense of interdependence value friendship and contribute to working towards common goals. They are able to give of themselves and they are able to receive assistance from others. They are altruistic. They influence and are influenced. Their intelligence is shaped through reciprocity with others.

When school leaders purposefully employ the three Ps of emotional intelligence in order to help colleagues illuminate their own internal resources as represented in the five states of mind, they build leadership capacity in others and enhance the organizational intelligence of their school.

> Group emotional intelligence is about small acts that make a big difference. It is not about a team member working all night to meet a deadline; it is about saying thank you for doing so. It is not about in-depth discussion of ideas; it is about asking a quiet member for his thoughts. It is not about harmony, lack of tension, and all members liking each other; it is about acknowledging when harmony is false, tension is unexpressed and treating others with respect.

Druskat and Wolff, 2001.

Collective emotional intelligence and mirror neurons

Emotions have been shown to be very contagious (Hatfield, 1994). We have only to recall a time when a disgruntled individual managed to derail a meeting or ruin a dinner party. Alternatively, we may recall how a cheerful person was able to lift a somber mood from a group. This is obviously as true in schools as it is in any other workplace.

Emotional contagion tends to flow from the most influential in a group to the least influential. So the emotions of the leader are important to the organization, just as the emotions of the teacher (usually the most influential in the classroom) are critical to student learning. A teacher who is disposed to cheerfulness and optimism will have a very different effect upon her students than a teacher who is chronically depressed.

There appears to be a neurological basis for the contagiousness of emotions. In the early 1990s scientists in Parma, Italy, discovered the existence of mirror neurons, cells in the brain that activate when we move and when we watch other people move. They appear to 'mirror' what we observe, giving us a clue as to how the process of imitative learning may take place.

Scientists have also linked mirror neurons to our emotional systems and these neurons may explain the contagious nature of emotions (Iacoboni, 2009). Through the use of brain imaging techniques, we are able to see that the emotional centers of our brain are activated not only when we make emotional facial expressions (anger, fear, repulsion, joy *etc*) but also when we see such expressions on the faces of other people.

The contagiousness of emotions suggests that in organizations or work groups there can come to exist a shared emotional climate and this can profoundly influence collective intelligence. The shared emotional climate can be either short term (for instance when a community goes into shared grief at the death of a member) or long term when a specific emotional culture blesses or haunts a school over many years.

Emotionally intelligent groups display the kind of cooperation, commitment and creativity that are critical for organizational effectiveness. Furthermore, while a collection of emotionally intelligent individuals does not guarantee a high functioning team, people who are members of emotionally intelligent groups tend to become more emotionally intelligent individuals. EQ, too, can be contagious.

School culture and narrative therapy

The psychologist Michael Thompson (2004) writes: 'It is impossible to spend any amount of time in small, independent schools without experiencing the emotional field they generate.' (p6)

It's worth spending a moment examining schools that have, over a number of years, become emotionally dysfunctional and have developed toxic cultures.

Thompson (2004) has applied the principles of narrative therapy to his consultancy work with emotionally troubled schools. He bases his work on the research of White and Epstein (1990). Their premise is that in order for an experience to be meaningful it must be 'storied' – it must be embedded in a narrative that we come to believe. According to Epstein and White, facts that are not 'storied' are lost from experience. Families share common narratives – some positive, some negative. Schools also come to share common narratives and these can have profound influences on the long-term emotional climate, organizational intelligence and become the very fabric of school culture.

These stories include networks of 'premises and presuppositions that constitute our maps of the world'. (Thompson, 2004, p2)

Dominant stories become just that: *dominant*. Thus alternative stories become crowded out or neglected and 'unique outcomes are lost because there is no intelligible framework into which they can fit and find meaning'. Negative dominant stories are both seductive and oppressive. They suck in positive-minded people, foster cynicism, spread suspicion and mistrust, encourage negative gossip and rumors and stifle optimism and efficacy. They are the nemesis of enhanced organizational intelligence.

We conduct professional development for teachers in between 25 and 30 schools each year. Fortunately the vast majority of them enjoy reasonably positive narratives. There are cultures of professional respect and trust. Occasionally, we will encounter a school that has developed a chronic negative narrative. The effect is immediately apparent – as it was in the International School of the Andaman Sea that was described in chapter one. The toxic culture pervades all aspects of the school and both organizational intelligence and student learning are impaired. The longer the negative narrative is allowed to dominate, the stronger it becomes and the more difficult it is to dislodge.

We all can think of schools that over years have developed reputations for being unpleasant places to work (these schools often attempt to compensate by offering high salaries, providing the so-called 'golden handcuffs' that only make the situation worse). These schools often have a high turnover of innovative leadership coupled with an entrenched faculty with a deep sense of entitlement. These are schools that tend to tell themselves negative collective stories.

Thompson suggests there are three steps in addressing a negative dominant narrative that has come to haunt a school:

Externalize the problem
Here we see the movement from subject to object, from the unspoken belief that *I* am the problem or *the school* is the problem to an external

source or cause. When we externalize the problem, we are no longer subject to it. We have objectified it outside of ourselves and therefore we have gained distance from it and may have some influence or control over it.

For example, in a school that is riddled with mistrust and suspicion, we might suggest that the external problem is 'fear'. We can ask questions such as when did fear invade our campus? What influence is fear having over our daily interactions? The process of externalizing the problem can mediate increased collective efficacy. Thompson talks about the process of 'unmasking' problems.

Map the influence of the problem in the life of the school
Collect the anecdotes from the members. Help the school paint a picture of what Fritz Perls (in Bandler & Grinder, 1979) would call the 'Existing State'. In order to get beyond the Existing State we need to honor it, but not to dwell on it. If we don't honor the problem, we will not appear to have taken it seriously. We can honor the problem by paraphrasing it – the emotion *first,* the content or substance of the issue *second.*

Map the influence of the school in the life of the problem
When we talk about the 'life' of the problem we are implying that, as with all living things, it has an end. We are also implying that the school is more resilient than the problem. We are inviting community members to move from being imprisoned in the Existing State towards a vision of the 'Desired State'. We can do this by asking for exceptionalities, what Pascale, Sternin & Sternin (2010) refer to as 'positive deviance'. Positive deviance is about learning from successful exceptions.

For example, we can ask whether there has ever been a time, when fear wasn't present in the school. What were the conditions under which fear was banished, even momentarily? Successful exceptions can also give us a road map for action, because 'It's easier to act your way into a new way of thinking, than to think your way into a new way of acting.' (Pascale *et al*, 2010, p38)

While Thompson (2004) writes from the perspective of a psychologist consultant going into support the healing of schools in conflict or crisis, we see a great relevance in narrative therapy for healthy schools – schools that strive to raise their collective intelligence.

How can teachers employ narrative strategies to influence and enhance school culture and organizational intelligence?

The mindset narratives

Mindsets are narratives that have to do with attribution theory (Dweck 2008). A person with a 'Fixed Mindset' believes that 'my successes or failures are attributable to factors outside my direct control' such as native intelligence, inherited talents, luck and task difficulty. A person with a 'Growth Mindset', on the other hand, attributes success or failure to factors within one's control such as effort, rehearsal or practice. In individuals, mindsets can be situational. We may believe that 'practice makes perfect' in music, but that 'I'm hopeless in mathematics.'

Fixed mindset narratives present a problem for both individuals and organizations. When an individual or an organization with a fixed mindset encounters failure it is likely to lead to a sense of learned helplessness: 'I just don't have the linguistic ability to learn French'. Or 'physics is just too hard'. In the case of an organization we might hear: "What did you expect with the administration ... teachers ...resources ... that we have here" or "we tried that already and it didn't work."

What is counter-intuitive is that Fixed Mindset narratives can also be disabling when we confront success. For example, when I attribute my success to factors beyond my control, such as native intelligence or natural talent, the possibility of failure becomes a threat to my very identity. If I fail, I will not be as intelligent as I believe I am. Fixed mindsets inhibit risk-taking and intellectual exploration.

When organizations develop collective fixed mindsets they also become risk-adverse. They will be reluctant to experiment with new ideas or innovate because such new ideas may bring mistakes and setbacks. Such failures are not perceived as learning opportunities but as a threat to the collective identity of the organization.

The International School of the Andaman Sea demonstrated such a fixed collective mindset. The headmaster recruited 'superstar teachers' whose native intelligence and natural teaching talent made the school the best in the world. The implication was that the faculty neither individually nor collectively had much control over these attributes. Native intelligence and natural talent are generally perceived to be inherited and therefore fixed. And so the invitation to engage in professional learning was actually perceived by many as a threat to identity – individually and collectively. If we need to learn, then it follows that we are not as good as we believe we are.

When we attribute success to forces outside our control, individuals and schools become risk adverse. An example of this might be when school leaders are reluctant to take a chance on the admission of a child with special learning needs and we hear them say, "We just don't have the resources" (the assumption being that those resources are fixed). In a similar situation, a growth mindset might be expressed as: "This child has specific learning needs that will provide both a challenge and an opportunity for our teachers. In what ways can we maximize learning for both the teachers and the child?"

School leaders need to work explicitly and self-consciously to develop collective growth mindsets. One way they can do so is by building multiple leadership succession plans. Each ascribed leader is expected to be mentoring his or her replacement. This is only possible when the moral imperative of the organization outweighs the vested self-interest of individuals.

The role of ascribed leadership

There is no question that ascribed school leaders (principals, directors and superintendents) need to be the architects of organizational culture. While teachers can and do have a powerful influence on culture, it is more challenging to improve culture without the active involvement of top leadership.

For example, at the height of the management crisis at the World Bank in 2006, 500 of the top executives were sent on a six-week leadership-training course specifically designed for them by Stanford and Harvard Universities. Only 37 did not attend: Paul Wolfowitz, the then president, six managing directors and 25 vice presidents. It is no wonder that the World Bank culture remained dysfunctional. Within a year Wolfowitz was ousted from his position.

We know that the relationship between employee and supervisor is a critical dimension in terms of staff retention and productivity. That relationship is a product of organizational emotional intelligence. A Gallup organization study of over two million employees at 700 companies found that both employee longevity and productivity was largely determined by the relationship with his or her supervisor (Zipkin, 2000). In a further study, Spherion and Louis Harris Associates (2000) found that employees who perceived that they had 'good bosses' were four times less likely to leave the company than those with supervisors who were perceived as 'poor'.

School leaders need to step back from the day-to-day focus on getting more and more done and instead focus on what is truly important. Carving out time each week for such activity seems to many an unaffordable luxury; only the most emotionally intelligent have the insight and determination to do so. Our next chapter looks specifically at how we manage time and space in order to become more collectively intelligent.

Guided study questions

What experiences have you had in your professional life with emotional contagion?

What is 'mediation' and how is it linked to building leadership capacity in others?

What are the three Ps of emotional intelligence? Which of these might be most useful for you to develop further? How will you go about doing so?

The authors suggest that when the Five States of Mind are in high resource effective teacher leadership emerges. Think of a colleague you are currently working with. What States of Mind are in high resource? Which States of Mind might need support? How might you facilitate that support?

In what areas of your life do you have Fixed Mindsets? In what areas do you have Growth Mindsets? How have these come into being? In what ways can we cultivate Growth Mindsets in our students and colleagues?

Reflective Conversation:
an opportunity to Practice the three Ps

Guidelines for the conversation: The purpose of this activity is to provide an opportunity for participants to practice the three Ps of emotional intelligence (pausing, paraphrasing and probing).

With a learning partner engage in a conversation that follows the question banks below. Each partner will have an opportunity to be the questioner and the respondent. Please designate each partner as either A or B.

Partner A will begin by asking the first five questions in sequence. After asking the questions, pause to provide your partner with a chance to think. Also pause for between three and five seconds after the response. Note what effect the pausing has on the flow of the conversation and on thinking. After a few responses, the questioner may want to paraphrase and then probe for greater clarity.

At the end of the first block of questions, Partner B takes on the role of the questioner (repeating the questions from the first block) and follows the instructions above.

Continue exchanging roles for each block of questions, remembering to practice pausing, paraphrasing and probing until time is called.

Reflecting upon your childhood, what was it about school that caused you the greatest enjoyment?

What were some of the most meaningful learning experiences either within or without the classroom?

Which teachers increased your commitment to learn and how did they go about it?

How would you describe the relationship that this teacher cultivated with his/her students?

What are some things that you learned from a teacher that he or she didn't explicitly teach?

How are you feeling right now? (You may want to ask this question whenever your partner seems to be showing pleasure or discomfort or just before you reverse roles at the end of a block of questions.)

Reverse roles. *(Reminder: The questioner asks, pauses, paraphrases and may inquire for clarity.)*

What are some beliefs and values that keep you in education?

What has recently caused you the greatest professional satisfaction?

What is the greatest professional challenge that you are currently facing?

What are you learning about yourself from this challenge?

Reverse roles. *(Reminder: The questioner asks, pauses, paraphrases and may inquire for clarity.)*

What professional goals do you have for yourself over the next five years?

What success indicators will you be looking for as you embark on this journey?

What specific strategies and approaches are you exploring in terms of reaching your goal?

Reverse roles.

Thinking about the current state of education, what worries you most?

If there was only one piece of advice you could offer a young person just entering the field of education, what might it be?

If there were one suggestion that you could make to your present head of school, what might that be?

What is most important to you about being a teacher?

What have you liked best about this reflective conversation?

This exercise was adapted from the *Cognitive Coaching Learning Guide*, originally designed for the Institute for Intelligent Behavior by William Baker and Stanley Shalit from Jones, J.E. & Jones J. (1992) *Dyadic encounter*, in *A Handbook of structured experiences for human relations training*. Iowa City, IA. University Associates.

Case study

Deciding what not to do

Donald Farrington had walked into a no man's land between a battle of Titans. The community was split down the middle as the results of the extraordinary general meeting showed. The vote of no confidence in the board of directors had been 356 to 364. The board had survived – by the skin of its teeth. There was no such split in the faculty – with only one or two exceptions, the teachers were unanimous in their anger, mistrust and suspicion of the board and 98% of them had signed the petition calling for the directors' resignation.

Like most catastrophes, the genesis of this one had been a small, seemingly insignificant event. A child with a learning disability had been removed from grade five. In its wisdom, the administration decided the middle school did not have an appropriate program for the child. The child's parents had appealed to the board. The board had initially backed the administration. The parents had gone to court and sued the school –naming individual administrators and board members in the suit. The board got cold feet and entered negotiations with the parents to settle the case out of court. The administration had attempted to rally the support of the staff.

Recognizing the absence of support on the part of the head of school, the board had summarily dismissed him and, accepting that there was no one to act in his place, had determined that for the rest of the school year, the school would be managed by a board committee. In the power vacuum, special interests soon emerged, including two board members who considered that the school desperately needed a house cleaning of ineffective teachers and the adoption of a merit pay system.

Fear and anger spread through the teaching community. Angry emails were exchanged. Generally sensible and gentle people accused each other of lying and deceit. Conspiracy theories sprung up like mushrooms in the shade. Malicious anonymous letters were sent and received. Newspaper articles appeared, quoting anonymous sources, giving biased reports of the conflict within the school.

Into this crucible walked the new head of school, Donald Farrington.

Success, Donald told his wife over breakfast on his first day of work, would be to survive in the job until Christmas. The teachers had degenerated into a lynch mob and three of the nine board members were certifiably insane.

The first board meeting of Donald's tenure was scheduled for his second day at work. The first part of the meeting was open to observers, the second was the executive session. To Donald's amazement the observers began to gather almost an hour before the meeting. By the time of the call to order the crowd had swollen to the point that the room could not hold it and the opening of the meeting was postponed until the venue could be changed to the theater.

Donald sensed the extraordinary tension and animosity in the air. He knew he would be called on to introduce himself. To fail to recognize the conflict would be disingenuous and might be perceived as cowardly. But how to go forward and what to say?

While the board chairman opened the meeting and went through the agenda and minutes of the previous meeting, Donald made notes to himself. The board chair called on Donald to introduce himself. There was silence in the room.

"It is customary when there is a new head of school for him to introduce himself by describing past accomplishments and providing a laundry list of what he will do in the future.

"I will do neither today. In fact, to the contrary, I will begin by stating categorically what I will not do. I will not serve as a referee in a boxing match between faculty and board. I will not serve as a judge determining guilty parties and handing out appropriate punishments. I will not attempt to determine blame and responsibility for the present crisis that besets the school. To do so would be to perpetuate the crisis and exacerbate the conflict. I will not take sides.

"Before the present crisis, this was a fine school. It will be a fine school once again.

"Now what will I do? I shall insure that the school refocusses itself on the education of children. The school is comprised of students, parents, teachers and board members. Each of you has an important role to play. But those roles have become confused. The teachers have become involved in politics. The board has become involved in the day-to-day management of the school. Role confusion has led to trespassing across boundaries. Frontiers of authority have been crossed; incursions have been made.

"Individuals and groups have been deeply offended. Some have felt threatened, others wounded. It is now time to move from the present obsession with political rumor and gossip, on getting even, on wreaking revenge and refocus on our core business – the education of our children.

"I call on everyone to stop the conflict, to cease fighting. I call on the teachers to get out of the politics of the school and get back to the business of teaching and learning. I call on the board to get out of the school management business and return to the legitimate business of school governance. I will accept and tolerate no less."

Donald sat down to a standing ovation and thunderous applause. Even the certifiably insane board members were on their feet.

Discussion questions

In what ways is Donald's approach to the crisis emotionally intelligent?

In what ways has Donald employed a 'growth mindset' approach?

In what ways does Donald's short speech represent leadership that has the potential for enhancing organizational intelligence?

Chapter 4

Working smarter, not harder

Teachers who strive after high quality learning for their students and themselves are incredibly hard working. In outstanding schools around the world it is not uncommon to find teachers at school ten to 12 hours a day, six or even seven days a week. They are preparing units of study, marking student work, engaging in professional development, leading field trips, coaching sports, planning service learning events, directing theatrical productions or rehearsing students for musical concerts.

These are the very teachers who, when something 'new' comes along, will ask: where will the time come from? They are understandably concerned with the multitudinous demands (many of them self-imposed) on their time and attention. *Where will the time come from?* It is a fair question that we will address.

As a child, Bill recalls his Aunt Grace attempting to coax him to dry the dinner dishes with the adage, 'Many hands make light work.' This is certainly true with physical labor such as drying dishes. It becomes more complex when the labor becomes cognitive as David Perkins (2003) points out in his 'lawn-mower paradox'. He suggests that it is much easier for six men to come together to mow a lawn than it is for six men to come together to design a lawn mower. However challenging it may be, collective cognitive labor is what makes organizations smarter.

In this chapter, we will argue that, by examining how we work together and by deliberately cultivating organizational intelligence, we can work smarter, not harder. We can increase our efficiency and effectiveness as educators without adding to the amount of time or energy that we commit to professional responsibilities.

The purpose of the chapter is to explore the relationship between organizational intelligence and how groups work together and process knowledge. The premise is that the quality of our working relationships will dramatically influence our collective intelligence and the caliber of our decision-making.

But first let's eavesdrop on a group of social studies teachers who are working smarter, not harder when they confront a common issue in culturally diverse schools:

English by osmosis?

Elaine Culley paused mid-sentence and bit her lip. There was silence in the social studies team room. Everyone waited for Elaine to continue. "I just don't know if I'm in the right job. I've got two new students today – one who has a learning disability and the other doesn't speak English."

"You're doing fine," Sally Henderson replied. "You've just had a hard day."

"I'm not doing fine!" Elaine snapped back. "You weren't there. It was awful. The kids just sat there. It was obvious that many of them didn't understand a word I was saying."

"You're feeling a bit overwhelmed," Clarissa Holder murmured sympathetically. She too had received some new ESL students.

"We all feel frustrated from time to time," Gabby Marcus added.

"I'm not feeling frustrated and it's more than being overwhelmed. I don't feel that I'm getting through to the kids. I don't know if I'm up to the job."

Elaine Culley was a first year teaching intern at Eudora International Academy. She had a *magna cum laude* degree from Dartmouth and outstanding recommendations. One of her letters of reference included the line: 'Elaine Culley is an outstanding scholar. She is absolutely meticulous in her planning. She is an extremely intelligent young woman who holds herself to a very high standard. I cannot recommend her too highly.'

But now the outstanding scholar was on the verge of tears in front of the entire department. Charles Barton, the chair of the social studies department, decided to intervene.

"It sounds as if you've had more than just a hard day. You're wondering if you are up to the job. Tell us more about what is specifically worrying you."

"I guess my self-confidence has been rattled. I think I'm OK with the English speakers. But now there are so many that don't speak English. I just don't know what to do with them. They just sit there and stare at me in silence. I don't have a clue what's going on in their minds."

Elaine paused before she continued.

"I just don't see how I can meet the needs of all the students. My class is up to 24 students and a full third are ESL kids. I'm all for inclusion in theory, but in practice it can be overwhelming."

"Elaine," Charles spoke slowly and seriously, commanding all of her attention. "What would your class look like if you were meeting the educational needs of all your students?"

Elaine didn't respond immediately, but Charles and the other members of the social studies department respected her thought process and remained silent.

"That's a hard question. What would my class look like when I'm meeting the educational needs of all my students?" Elaine repeated the question and bit the edge of her index finger. "I guess I'd like to see all the kids on task with their assignments. And for the most part they are. We've got really good kids."

Elaine used a handkerchief to dab the moist corners of her eyes. "I've been giving the ESL kids modified assignments. I'm not sure it's the right thing to do, but I didn't think they would be able to cope…"

Elaine stopped mid sentence. Again her colleagues respected her silence.

"You know what is really difficult," Elaine announced slowly. "It's when the new ESL kids don't say anything. I don't have any idea how much they understand. I don't have any idea if I'm actually teaching them anything or I'm just talking to myself. Sometimes I think we're just there wasting each other's time."

"You're worried about wasting valuable learning time," Charles said.

"I am! I don't know if they're learning anything."

"You're not sure what the silence of the new ESL students means and it worries you."

"It does worry me. I'm not a trained ESL teacher!"

"If you were in their place – a new student in a new school who doesn't speak English – what might be some of your thoughts?"

Elaine was quiet for several seconds. "I suppose I'd be feeling a bit insecure."

"You think they might be lacking in self-confidence?"

Elaine looked up at Charles sharply. Her eyes widened. "You mean like me?"

Charles smiled and said nothing.

"You mean that the ESL kids are feeling as nervous and insecure as I am? I hadn't thought of that. I need to find a way to put them at ease. No wonder they're quiet. I guess I'd be quiet too. I mean I know that receptive language has to develop before expressive language. Maybe there are some other ways for them to show me that they have understood a lesson."

"What do you have in mind?"

"Maybe I could use more non-verbal activities with them. Maybe I could develop some visual cues or symbols."

"A simple sign language?"

"Exactly. Maybe I could take the ESL kids as a group for a short meeting and we could develop a secret sign language so that they could let me know when they don't understand without any embarrassment."

"I suspect the ESL kids would really appreciate your concern for them," Charles added, noting Elaine's eyes were now dry and rather bright.

Charles Barton, as the social studies department chair, practiced the three Ps of emotional intelligence and engaged Elaine in structured reflective inquiry. He offered her no advice, no solutions, no autobiographical scenarios and no evaluation. He assumed that Elaine had the resources to resolve her own issues and provided the support (by pausing, paraphrasing and probing) that allowed her to develop her own way forward. Charles' collegial leadership through coaching enhanced the group's intelligence.

Historically, teaching has been a very lonely and isolated profession. However, increasingly schools are recognizing that collectively we have much greater potential to improve student learning than when we work in isolation. Collaboration, like many over-used words in education, evokes many things to many people and has been misused as a synonym for cooperation, conviviality, and collegiality.

We see collaboration taking place when members of a learning community work together as equals – irrespective of positions of authority – towards a common goal. Partnerships in collaborative relationships may be between students as they work in groups, between students and teachers, and between teachers as they work to assist students to succeed in the classroom.

Collaboration is based on mutual goals and shared responsibility for both participation and decision-making. Individuals who collaborate share accountability for outcomes (Cook & Friend, 1991; Kusuma-Powell & Powell, 2000). Collaboration is the norm in high performing and improving schools and results in increased student achievement. However, collaborations skills need to be taught explicitly (Garmston & Wellman, 2009).

Before we look at the specific skills that we need to develop in terms of professional collaboration, let's go back to two critical environmental influences on how teachers work together: time and task management; and the design of our contact architecture.

But where will the time come from?

Over two hundred years ago, Goethe wrote (in Knox, 1998) that 'things that matter least must never be at the mercy of things that matter most'. Easier said than done – particularly in our very demanding and busy schools. However, we would argue that the quantity of time, in and of itself, is not the sole issue. How we use time is at the heart of the matter. In order to manage our time and tasks effectively, we need to start with the end in mind. We need to ask ourselves what are our really important goals. For without a destination, it doesn't matter which road we take.

Steven Covey (2004) suggests that one way to organize and prioritize our thinking about time and task management is to distinguish between the 'urgent' and the 'important'. In the figure below the vertical columns represent the urgent and the not urgent. The horizontal rows represent the important and the not important. We have created four quadrants into which most of our professional activities can fit. Let's examine each of these quadrants in turn:

Time and task management matrix

	URGENT	**NOT URGENT**
IMPORTANT	**Quadrant 1** Crises Deadline driven projects Pressing Issues and Problems Health and Safety issues Example: Have fire the alarms repaired	**Quadrant 2** Personal professional learning Preventative activities Relationship building Recognizing new opportunities Planning Professional inquiry Recreation Example: Think about what second language should be taught in the primary school
NOT IMPORTANT	**Quadrant 3** Interruptions Some phone calls, e-mails, social networking Some meetings Popular activities Proximate, pressing activities Example: Meet a deadline for a submission to the weekly school newsletter	**Quadrant 4** Trivia Some mail Some calls, e-mail Time wasters Examples: Decide on appropriate plants to decorate the reception area Play a video game

Quadrant 1 is the home of the crisis manager. The activities we would find in Quadrant 1 are both urgent and important. Some examples might include meeting important deadlines, health and safety issues, or replacing a teacher who goes on sudden medical leave. There is no question that teachers and school leaders will inevitably spend some of their professional time in Quadrant 1.

However, if we dwell too long in Quadrant 1 the results are counterproductive and we see the effects of chronic crisis management –

stress and possible burn-out. Quadrant 1 is ironically seductive and can easily become the home of the 'teacher leader as savior/martyr' or 'leader as hero'.

Educators who spend most of their time in Quadrant 1 are deadline driven producers and crisis managers. They tend to be reactive in that they see problems as opposed to opportunities. The longer we stay in Quadrant 1, the more it can come to dominate our life.

Quadrant 3 is the home of other peoples' pressing issues. These can be pet peeves, hobby-horses and the special interests of individuals or groups. The urgency is external to self and the activities are not important, but the pressure can be immense.

Quadrant 3 can often emerge when teachers or school leaders take on problems and issues that are not rightfully their own. They may do so from the best of intentions, but the activities of Quadrant 3 reflect the expectations and priorities of other people. The urgency of Quadrant 3 may seem all too real, but the activities and issues simply aren't important in the greater life of the school. The teacher who spends a great deal of time in Quadrant 3 is constantly putting out fires – other peoples' conflagrations.

Time pressure, the sense of urgency we feel, has been shown to have a strong influence on our behavior. The classic research in this field is referred as The Good Samaritan Experiment. Researchers Darley and Batson (in Zimbardo & Boyd, 2008) investigated how individual Princeton seminary students might behave in preparation for giving a brief sermon on the Good Samaritan.

The seminarians were told that the sermon was to be presented at a building across the campus and that it would be evaluated by their supervisors. The stakes were reasonably high. As each individual completed his preparation, he was told EITHER that he was late and he must hurry to the prescribed sermon venue OR that he had plenty of time but he might as well head over now. The only difference in the two groups was the manipulation of their sense of urgency.

As the seminarians walked across the campus, each encountered a person slumping over in an alleyway in obvious great physical distress (an accomplice of the researchers). The seminarians were faced with the decision of whether to assist the stranger – as the Biblical Good Samaritan had done – or to hurry to their presentation. The question that interested the researchers was whether time pressure would influence the students' behavior. Specifically, would *doing* the right thing take precedence over giving a sermon *about* the right thing?

The sense of urgency felt by the seminarians had a profound effect on their behavior. The vast majority who believed they had plenty of time stopped to assist the stranger in distress. However, over 90% of the students who believed they were late for their presentation failed to render assistance. Darley and Batson's seminal research demonstrates that time perspectives change people's behavior (Zimbardo & Boyd, 2008, p16.) so that they may act in ways that are counter to their deeply held beliefs and values.

For this reason we need to be doubly cautious about activities that dwell in Quadrants 1 and 3: urgency can blind us to real ethical and moral concerns.

Given that the pressure of time is one of the most frequently-cited obstacles to school improvement initiatives, it is useful to recognize that an acute sense of urgency, particularly over a prolonged period of time, can have disturbing influences on our moral compass and even our common sense.

Covey (2004) tells the story of a lumberjack in a forest feverishly working to saw down a large tree. The man was exerting enormous effort, perspiring profusely and yet making little progress. After a few minutes, Covey interrupted the lumberjack and suggested that he might pause and sharpen his saw. The irritated man replied that he was too busy cutting down the tree to stop and sharpen his saw. In schools too, a prevailing sense of urgency can blind us to what may be obvious to outside observers. Hard work may demand appreciation, but effort is never a substitute for effectiveness.

Quadrant 4 includes activities that are neither urgent nor important. A ruthless self-evaluation of our daily professional lives may reveal several of these. The results of spending too much time in either Quadrant 3 or 4 is irresponsibility. Effective educators stay out of quadrants 3 and 4 because, urgent or not, the activities simply aren't important.

Quadrant 2 is the place to be where our professional activities are important but not urgent. Why not urgent? Urgency implies that we need to deal with something immediately and that our actions are reactive. Quadrant 2 is about vision and perspective, self-discipline and balance. It includes planning, locating opportunities, preventative maintenance, and building a school culture of trust. It includes doing things that will enhance student learning – activities that often get crowded out of our overly busy professional lives.

Quadrant 2 requires us to be in touch with our core educational values and beliefs and to carve out time to engage in activities that reflect those values and beliefs. But to say yes to Quadrant 2 activities, we have to learn how to say no to other pressing demands on our time.

Developing memories of the future

Quadrant 2 is future-oriented. David Ingvar, a psychologist from Lund University in Sweden (de Geus, 1997) has written about how people develop 'time paths', contingency plans that are relevant to our future. For example, if my proposal is ready this afternoon, I'll be able to get it printed and submit it before the deadline. If it isn't, I'll need to request an extension of time. The best person to ask for such an extension would be…

Ingvar suggests that by developing these time paths we create what he refers to as 'memories of the future'. These serve to sensitize us so that we are able to recognize opportunities for pro-active adaptation, thus underscoring the truth of the old adage that fortune favors the prepared mind. The more memories of the future we construct, the more likely we are to recognize and capitalize on future opportunities. Dealing with the future can never be delegated. Memories of the future are constructed in Quadrant 2.

This brings us of the concept of 'opportunity costs'. When we invest time in one activity, we forego investing time in another. In other words to say yes to activity A is to say no to B. Time investment needs to be a deliberate decision. Zimbardo and Boyd (2008) suggest that opportunity costs are beyond simple cost-benefit analysis because the metaphor tends to treat time as a tangible commodity, which, of course, it is not.

We can't save time, purchase it, borrow it or steal it. We can't store it for a rainy day. We can't even waste it. We can, however, develop a sensitivity to our perception of temporal duration. Accordingly Zimbardo reminds us of the Great Law of the Iroquois: 'In every deliberation we must consider the impact on the seventh generation ... even if it requires having skin as thick as the bark of a pine.' (p181)

Many teachers begin their school day by making a list of things to do. An interesting twist on this is to start each day making a list of things NOT to do. Often deciding on what we are not going to do will actually allow us to carve out time for important Quadrant 2 activities.

Contact architecture: the structure of our iteraction

The structure of our physical and social environment can have a profound impact on the collective intelligence of the group or organization.

A number of years ago, the board of directors of an international school in Africa allocated a substantial amount of money for the complete refurbishment of the science labs. The head of the science department presented Bill, who was the new high school principal, with the floor plan design for three labs. A great deal of care had been taken in preparing the drawings. They were drawn to scale with different colors representing the different services (*eg* water, electricity, gas) and there was a clear focus on student safety. Fire blankets, emergency showers and fume cabinets were all in place.

What concerned Bill was that student work-stations were constructed in fixed rows, all anchored to the floor and all facing the whiteboard at the front of the room. Bill asked what effect this arrangement might have on teaching and learning. The head of the science department responded that he thought it would be very conducive to teaching and learning since all students would be facing the front of the room and that was where the teacher usually positioned himself.

At a conference some weeks later, Bill showed the lab design to a female biology teacher from a different school. Her first reaction was to chuckle and ask if a *man* had designed the floor plan. After Bill had confirmed the gender of the designer, she suggested it was a very male design in that boys tend to have shoulder-to-shoulder relationships – they socialize while they are engaged in an activity (computer games, sports, car mechanics *etc*).

Girls, on the other hand, tend to have more face-to-face friendships that involve conversation. The rigid design of lab work-stations prevented students from having face-to-face interactions with each other. It assumed that all learning would come from the front of the room – the teacher.

A series of discussions followed that used the design of the science labs as a springboard to explore some deeply-held assumptions about teaching and learning. For example, the design proposed by the head of the science department had all the students facing the teacher. What did this suggest about the role of the teacher? Was the teacher seen to be the traditional dispenser of information and knowledge? Were the students somehow cast into the role of passive recipients? What were the implications of the work-station design for instructional pedagogy?

The design lent itself to traditional lectures and demonstrations. Students could work in pairs, shoulder to shoulder, but cooperative learning groups were virtually impossible as was any student-to-student inquiry. Did the rigid contact architecture of the proposed design suggested that the teacher didn't expect students to learn very much from each other? Did the design actually inhibit student critical thinking?

We believe that not only the physical environment but also our attitudes towards the space in which we work, our contact architecture, can have a profound impact on our collective intelligence.

Furniture in war and peace

There may be interesting cultural dimensions to contact architecture. In March 1968 the United States and North Vietnam entered into peace talks in Paris designed to end the Vietnam War. For over a month, the talks focused solely on what shape table the negotiators should sit around. The United States favored a rectangular table at which the adversaries could be seated on opposite sides, clearly delineating the opposing points of view.

The North Vietnamese, on the other hand, favored a round table at which all parties could come as 'equals'. The western press ridiculed the impasse. When so many lives were at stake, how absurd was it to argue over the shape of a piece of furniture?

The question was probably designed to be rhetorical, but we enjoy trying to answer rhetorical questions – on occasion interesting insights emerge.

Richard Nisbett (2003) suggests that culture influences the way in which we think; the way in which we make sense out of the world; and, the way in which we learn. He asserts Asian and Westerners think and learn differently.

For Nisbett, it is no accident that algebra was developed in ancient Greece and geometry in China. Western intellectual tradition has prized dichotomous and reductionist thinking. The experimental sciences were developed in the west and these have their basis in syllogistic thinking. If X, then not Y. We have in the west the development of a precedent based system of jurisprudence in which there is the assumption that adversarial confrontation will, more often than not, reveal a version of the truth beyond a reasonable doubt.

In the Far East, on the other hand, there is less dichotomous and reductionist thinking. There is greater attention to both the foreground and the background of issues. Truth is perceived to be more complex and perhaps more illusive. There is less 'either/or' thinking and more emphasis on a search for a middle way. de Bono (1991) calls this 'water logic' as opposed to 'rock logic'.

The prolonged argument over the shape of the table at the Paris Peace Talks may well have had its roots in the culturally different ways of thinking of the negotiators. Anecdotally, we have always found conversation richer when participants in a workshop (or dinner guests) are seated at a round table.

A milestone in western organizational intelligence
David Perkins (2003) cites the mythic court of Camelot as a milestone in the development of western organizational intelligence. It is not the bravery of the Arthurian knights or their chivalry that he has in mind, but rather the shape of King Arthur's round table. Why, we ask, should a seventh-century piece of furniture occupy such a revered place in intellectual history?

Before Camelot, royal tables were rectangular and very long. The monarch sat at the far end, usually on a raised dais or plinth. Retainers were seated along each side of the table in rank order of their power and influence. Thus a nobleman seated at the far end of the rectangular table was beyond the reach of the king's ear and as such had very little power or influence.

As you can imagine, the seating plan for royal tables was almost always an issue of controversy and conflict. Geoffrey of Monmouth, in his 12th century *Historia Regum Britanniae*, asserts that the seating plan of an Arthurian yuletide feast erupted into such violence that Arthur commissioned a Cornish carpenter to build an enormous, but easily transportable, round table so as to prevent further disputes.

And so the legendary King Arthur was able to bring together fractious warlords and unite England for the first time – not through force or compulsion, but by improving the contact architecture – the structure of interaction.

Traditional contact architecture: Egg crate schools

Traditionally schools have been designed along a pattern similar to an egg crate (Lortie, 1975). Egg crates are great for transporting eggs, insulating them to prevent their cracking in transit. Egg crates are a much less satisfactory model for schools.

In such schools, adults are physically, socially and professionally isolated from each other; there is little purposeful relationship building; and collaboration happens, if at all, by accident. Such isolation is the enemy of school improvement and stands as a major obstacle to raising organizational intelligence.

Nevertheless many, perhaps even most, schools still resemble egg crates. Fullan (2001) writes: 'over the years schools have built up all kinds of structural and cultural barriers to sharing, and they are having a devil of a time overcoming the inertia. (If they weren't so well protected by having nearly a monopoly, and if they weren't so essential to the future of democracy, they would be long gone.)' (p99)

Bill recalls his first day as a teacher at a public high school north of New York City. The chairman of the English department introduced him to his colleagues by saying that he would be working with very highly educated and experienced teachers who shared a common parking lot. And that was about all teachers did share in those days – a common parking lot and, in the winter, the heating system.

Intelligent organizations don't just generate and use data, they create knowledge. Knowledge creation only takes place in a social context (Fullan 2001). There is no school improvement initiative that will be successful if it doesn't also improve relationships with the organization.

Contact architecture is the purposeful structuring of professional interaction and is critical to relationship-building. If the schedule of the working day isolates teachers from one another, there will be no opportunity for teachers to build professional relationships. If teachers perceive their work space as personal property, territoriality will emerge and teaching practice will remain privatized. If teachers are not provided with time during the school day to forge professional relationships, they will not happen. No amount of lip service to collaboration will overcome a poor contact architecture.

Can a robin become a titmouse?

Alan Wilson, a professor of biology at the University of California at Berkeley, became interested in the contact architecture, the structure of interaction and learning, in two species of British garden birds: robins and titmice (de Geus, 1997; Perkins, 2003). The background to his research is fascinating.

Milk deliveries began in Britain in the late 19th century. Horse-drawn carts would leave the local dairies before first light in the morning and the milk man would place the bottles of milk on the recipients' doorsteps. Back then the milk bottles did not have caps and both the robins and titmice soon learned how to perch on the tops of bottles and drink the rich cream that had settled at the top.

In the 1930s the British dairies began sealing the milk bottles with aluminum caps. There can be no question that this innovation improved the milk's cleanliness and prevented spills and it should have thwarted the avian milk thieves. But it didn't. Soon both robins and titmice learned to peck through the aluminum caps and drink the cream anyway.

Over the years, it became obvious that there were many, many more titmice milk snitchers than there were robins. In fact by the 1950s there was hardly a titmouse in greater London that wasn't conversant with the milk bottle caper.

Alan Wilson asked himself the question: what was it about the titmice that allowed innovative practice to spread more rapidly through their species in comparison to the robins? Wilson's research analyzed how the specific contact architecture, the structure of interaction, can nourish or inhibit the growth of learning and collective intelligence.

Wilson recognized that the first step in spreading innovative practice is that an individual has to make the break through. From his research he learned that both robins and titmice had such discoverers in approximately equal numbers. So, in terms of individual creativity, there was not much between the two species. However, to connect this to organizational intelligence we need to examine the contact architecture of robin and titmouse societies.

The robin society has a poor structure of interaction for group learning, while the titmouse society has an excellent one for the spreading of innovative practices. Robins are territorial. They plot out their personal domains and defend their boundaries. In contrast, titmice are collectively nomadic. They travel in small foraging flocks with frequent changes in membership.

This meant that when a robin discovered how to peck though the aluminum cap, other robins usually didn't learn about it. On the other hand, when a titmouse made the same discovery other titmice would see and learn. The flock rotation increased the contagiousness of learning and raised the collective intelligence of the species.

This may be one of the reasons that renaissances in human progress, prior to the internet age, occurred in urban rather than rural areas. The contact architecture for creativity and innovation was simply better in the urban environment.

We often share Alan Wilson's research with participants in workshops on teacher collaboration. On one such occasion, a participant demanded to know if a robin could become a titmouse. She was, of course, speaking metaphorically. It was an intriguing question. Can profoundly territorial teachers move beyond the safety of the egg crate? Can pedagogical robins be transformed into effective collaborators and constructive team members?

Moving from personal EQ to social intelligence in the math department

Kevin was asking the same question. Can a teacher robin become a teacher titmouse? Kevin was the chair of the math department at a large international school in South America. With a high degree of emotional competence, Kevin is aware of his emotions and is fairly skilled at managing them.

However, as chair of the math department, Kevin has to lead a group of much less emotionally-mature individuals. He needs not only personal emotional competence, but also social intelligence – that is an awareness and management of the emotions of others.

Kevin accomplished this social intelligence by establishing explicit norms that encourage interpersonal understanding. These norms describe the behaviors that group members will be exhibiting when they are actively listening and attempting to understand each other's ideas and feelings. Kevin found that once the norms were established, the more retiring and reserved team members felt a greater willingness to participate in group conversations.

Kevin found that his department needed norms for both caring and confronting. He found that the norms for caring were relatively easy to establish. These included displays of positive regard, appreciation, and respect. He identified these norms as expressed through behavior that reflected support, validation and compassion.

Kevin's team members found the norms of confrontation more challenging to establish, although they recognized intuitively that there were vitally important to their work as a team. Chapter seven provides a deeper examination of how the norms of confrontation, the management of conflict, may differ in schools at different stages of collective development.

So we return to the question of whether a territorial robin can become a collaborating titmouse? We believe the answer is yes, but the specific norms of collaboration need to be explicitly taught and regularly practiced. Norms are behaviors that we practice on a regular basis so that they become habitual. There are seven norms of collaborative work (Garmston and Wellman, 2009). The first three are the same as the three Ps of emotional intelligence: pausing, paraphrasing and probing.

The seven norms of collaborative work

Pausing: Pausing before responding or asking a question allows time for thinking and enhances dialogue, discussion and decision-making.

Paraphrasing: Using a paraphrase starter that is comfortable for you: "So..." or "As you are..." or "You're thinking..." and following the starter with a paraphrase assists members of the group to hear and understand each other as they formulate decisions.

Probing: Using gentle open-ended probes or inquiries such as: "Please say more…" or "I'm curious about…" or "I'd like to hear more about…" or "Then, are you saying…?" increases the clarity and precision of the group's thinking.

Putting ideas on the table: Ideas are the heart of a meaningful dialogue. Label the intention of your comments. For example, you might say, "Here is one…" or "One thought I have is…" or "Here's a possible approach…"

Paying attention to self and others: Meaningful dialogue is facilitated when each group member is conscious of self and of others and is aware of not only what she/he is saying but how it is said and how others are responding.

This includes paying attention to learning styles when planning for, facilitating and participating in group meetings. Responding to others in their own language forms is one manifestation of this norm.

Presuming positive presuppositions: Assuming that other's intentions are positive promotes and facilitates meaningful dialogue and eliminates unintentional put-downs. Using positive presuppositions in your speech is one manifestation of this norm.

Putting inquiry at the center: The purpose of inquiry is to enhance collective understanding. It follows a pattern of pausing, paraphrasing and probing for clarity and specificity. It moves a group beyond data and information towards the generation of applicable knowledge and, on occasion, wisdom.

Adapted from *The Adaptive School: Developing and Facilitating Collaborative Groups* (2001) by Robert Garmston and Bruce Wellman, Christopher Gordon Publisher.

By regularly practicing the seven norms of collaboration, groups can re-invent their collective culture. Each norm is 'other-centered' in that it focuses on supporting the thinking of another person. The norms also serve to build relationships, to foster an inclusive sense of belonging, and to enhance the groups' deep understanding of an issue or idea. Each of the norms is respectful and serves to strengthen the fabric of group trust.

So, in a results-oriented era such as the present, do we really have time for such 'soft' options? We often hear this question from people outside education – well-intentioned and impatient school reformers.

First, these aren't options. Trust is not a soft option that schools can opt in or out of. When schools experience an absence of trust, suspicion, mistrust, fear, gossip and rumors rush in to fill the vacuum. As anyone who has worked in such a toxic culture can attest: student learning is unquestionably harmed (Bryk & Schneider, 2005; Tschannen-Moran, 2004). Trust in schools is non-negotiable, but very little time is spent explicitly examining how it is established and maintained and, at times, repaired.

Secondly, 'soft' data is often dismissed or disparaged because it is not easily quantified. There is a narrow-minded assumption that accountability must be associated with numbers. This is a mental and moral *cul de sac*.

We know what happens to ethical behavior when we become obsessed with 'making our numbers'. Witness Enron and the unfortunate number of school districts in the United States that have been mired in standardized test cheating scandals. Defining accountability solely in terms of quantifiable 'hard' data leads us to measure only that which is easily measureable. When we do so, we take the soul out of education.

In his classic work *Improving Schools from Within,* Roland Barth (1990) asserts that one of the most accurate barometers to the quality of student learning that is going on in the classroom is the quality of the adult-to-adult relationships within the schoolhouse. He urges us to examine how teachers treat each other, learn from each other, share craft knowledge, encourage each other, solve problems or manage conflicts. These elements reflect very accurately the quality of the learning experience students have in the classroom and define organizational intelligence.

Fullan (2010) refers to 'collective capacity' as the power of an effective group to do what no one individual could possibly achieve. He writes that the power of collective capacity is that it enables ordinary people to accomplish extraordinary things, for two reasons. One is that knowledge about effective practice becomes widely available on a daily basis. The second is more powerful still: working together generates commitment. Moral purpose, when it stares you in the face through students and your peers working together to make lives and society better is palpable, indeed virtually irresistible. The speed of effective change increases exponentially.

All productive schools have a fabric of collaboration and trust. Some take that culture for granted and for this reason are highly vulnerable organizations. We see this time and time again when a school that has been doing well experiences a change of personnel in terms of the school board or leadership; fear and mistrust emerge. In great schools, educators pay self-conscious attention to school culture. Teachers come to perceive themselves as the stewards and guardians of the collective trust. These schools are much less fragile and therefore are more likely to weather change constructively.

Guided study questions

In what specific ways do the authors suggest that teachers can work smarter, not harder?

What criteria would you use in placing an activity in Quadrant 2?

What are some specific Quadrant 2 activities that you and your department or team could engage in?

What are some characteristics of highly collaborative groups?

What elements of 'contact architecture' might be inhibiting or enhancing collaboration in your school?

Which of the seven norms of collaboration will you or your team be working to develop?

Time and task management matrix

Below please find a time and task matrix. Individually or with your team enter examples from your daily professional life that fit within the four quadrants. Once you have done so, explore the quadrants looking for patterns. What insights are emerging?

	URGENT	NOT URGENT
IMPORTANT	**Quadrant 1** Crises Deadline driven projects Pressing Issues and Problems Health and Safety issues Examples: 1. 2. 3. 4.	**Quadrant 2** Personal professional learning Preventative activities Relationship building Recognizing new opportunities Planning Professional inquiry Recreation Examples: 1. 2. 3. 4.
NOT IMPORTANT	**Quadrant 3** Interruptions Some phone calls, e-mails, social networking Some meetings Popular activities Proximate, pressing activities Examples: 1. 2. 3. 4.	**Quadrant 4** Trivia Some mail Some calls, e-mail Time wasters Examples: 1. 2. 3. 4.

Construct a NOT to do list

Individually or with your team, brain storm a list of Quadrant 3 and 4 activities that you would like to stop doing. What have the items in common? What are your hunches about why you remain attracted to these activities?

The Dot Game

The Dot Game is a simple simulation that brings home some of the challenges that groups face in collaboration and building organizational intelligence. We have used the Dot Game with groups as large as 100 although 30 is probably an ideal number. Numbers below ten are probably too low for the game to be effective. The Dot Game usually takes no more than about 15 minutes.

You will need to prepare small slips of paper – one for each participant. Three quarters of the slips are blank; one quarter have large black dots in the center. Distribute the folded slips to the participants with the instruction NOT to show their paper to anyone else. Explain that some will be blanks and some will have dots.

If yours is a blank, you must tell the truth. If you have a dot, you may lie. The objective of the game is for the blanks to form the largest non-dot group, and for the dots to infiltrate non-dot groups. Individuals and groups develop strategies for determining whether someone is a dot.

If someone is accused of being a dot, he or she must leave that group immediately even if they are not a dot. The accused may then attempt to join another group. After six or seven minutes, the facilitator calls time and asks to see the hands of the people who were accused of being dots but were not. The facilitator asks these individuals how that felt. The facilitator then asks to see the hands of the real dots.

The facilitator asks the participants to return to their table groups and in small groups discuss the following reflective question: what real life challenges does the dot game present that collaborating teachers need to address?

Some possible themes that emerge might include: the importance of being included (Maslow's hierarchy); how aggressive behavior can be a mask for insecurity; how reputations can follow an individual from one group to another; or how first impressions can be misleading.

Organizational simulation and reflection

The facilitator explains to the participants (in groups of five or six) that they will now have a chance to practice their collaboration skills. In their teams they will be building a rocket. They will have 15 minutes of planning time, 15 minutes of building and 15 minutes of judging and reflection. Explain that the criteria for the perfect rocket is as follows:

The rocket must look like a rocket
The rocket must be free standing – not attached to anything
The rocket must be at least 5'8" or 1.7 meters high
The rocket must be able to withstand a moderate breeze
on takeoff

The facilitator then invites one participant from each table to collect their building material. Teams may not use anything other than the materials provided, which include:

One piece of flipchart paper
Three pieces of 8.5in x 11in or A4 paper
Two paper plates
Three paper cups
Three drinking straws
One pair of scissors
One roll of masking tape
Two paper clips
One colored marker

The facilitator reminds participants that, during the planning period, the team members may not touch the actual building material.

During the planning period, the facilitator circulates throughout the room observing each group to see what leadership emerges. At the end of the planning period, the facilitator indicates that the teams can start building. About 90 seconds into the building period, the facilitator moves one person (the person who has been identified during the planning period as a leader) to another group. So each table groups loses a member and gains a new member. Groups are not warned before that this will happen.

At the end of the building period, the rockets are moved to the 'launch pad' and judged to see if they meet the specified criteria. The facilitator is the 'moderate breeze'. Following the judging, participants are asked to return to their table groups (those who were moved stay with their building groups) and enter into a Round Robin Reflection.

Round robin reflection

Table group members number off.

Person number one then answers two questions:

> What decisions did I make about how, whether and when I would participate in the previous activity in relation to the norms of collaboration?

> In what ways did my participation affect others in the group?

Person two paraphrases person one's remarks and then answers the same two questions.

There are no interruptions or cross talk.

Person three paraphrases person two and then answers the two questions.

Repeat the pattern until all table group members have had a turn.

Note: The facilitator may wish to process with the large group the feelings of the individuals who were moved and how they were received by their new groups. He or she may also want to ask: how this simulation is like our real life in schools?

Case study
The writing on the wall

Sarah loved metaphors, but she recognized that she was mixing them up. She knew it as a sign of stress. She wondered if the writing on the wall was a tempest in a teapot or a molehill becoming a mountain or perhaps a giant energy trap. Could the ugly duckling become a beautiful swan?

Her many years experience as elementary principal told her not to underestimate the explosive potential of seemingly minor issues. She felt a little as though she was sitting on a powder keg or maybe it was a tinder box. There she went again with the silly metaphors.

She also knew that she had to remain emotionally uninvolved. That shouldn't be too difficult. She couldn't understand how people could get this worked up over children's handwriting.

But worked up they were. Beth and Marianne in grade two had manned the barricades in defense of Zaner-Bloser Script while Carolyn in grade three was on a soap box about how most schools used the D'Nealian approach. A parent had emailed a critique of both and had recommended Getty-Dubay. An anonymous donor had left a copy of *Handwriting Without Tears* on her desk and Ann and Dorothy were passionate apostles of something called *Real Script*.

Sarah was aware that there was no consistency in the elementary school in respect to how handwriting was taught. Some teachers used one system, some another, and some didn't seem to use any system as at all.

This state of affairs might have been acceptable if children were developing legible handwriting and if teachers weren't so rigid in their approach. However, neither seemed to be the case. There had been two parent complaints about teachers forcing children to change from one system to another – essentially compelling children with reasonable handwriting to relearn how to form and join their letters!

Sarah also recognized other aspects of the situation. First, that emotions and passionate advocacy were clouding and confusing the issues. Second, that almost all children learn to write by one system or another – so that one handwriting system was probably not a quantum degree better than another. Third, that the factions needed to be heard. And fourth, and perhaps most importantly, the goal was no one particular handwriting program, but rather *consistency of approach*.

Sarah invited representatives of the different advocacy groups to prepare written statements of no more than 1000 words on why the school should adopt their choice of handwriting programs. The briefs were compiled and distributed to the faculty. Each group was then invited to make a 20-minute presentation to a full faculty meeting. At the conclusion of the meeting the faculty were asked to analyze the presentations (NOT to make a recommendation) in terms of the relative strengths and weaknesses of the different approaches. Sarah then summarized the teachers' analyses and circulated the summary to the faculty and parents.

A month later, Sarah met the grade level team leaders and reviewed the teacher analyses of the different handwriting approaches. Within 40 minutes they had come to consensus that the school should adopt *Real Script*. Sarah was surprised at the outcome but the reasons were sound and the benefits were obvious to all. Sarah put out a memo to the staff and a letter to the parents describing the process and the outcome.

There were a few disappointed teachers and parents, but by and large everyone understood the process and could live with the outcome. It had been a successful outcome. Sarah searched for a metaphor. It was not enough to break eggs, she thought to herself, you have to inspire them towards omelette-hood.

Discussion questions

In terms of the Time and Task Matrix, into which quadrant would you place the search for a consistent handwriting approach? Why?

What values and beliefs guide Sarah's handling of the situation?

What norms of collaboration has she employed?

Chapter 5

The power of collaborative inquiry

Groups have the potential for being intelligent by paying attention to different aspects of their individual and collective interaction. Margaret Wheatley (2006) was one of the first writers to draw connections between the new field of 'complexity theory' in science and the ways and means of how humans behave and collectively organize themselves.

She suggests that combining quality information with quality interaction and then identifying and extracting promising patterns produces peer culture or group identity. The process produces shared understandings and values, celebrations of evidence-based successes and releases additional energy for organizational improvement. Such can be the power of collaborative inquiry. Arguably, the most important dimensions to group knowledge processing are first being present and focused and then being deliberate and intentional in how we speak to one another.

Being present and focused has to do with setting aside distractions. The distractions may be external to self (sleepless technology, urgent but unimportant demands on our attention, high maintenance colleagues, *etc*) or they can be internal (stressors such as job-related worries, familial or financial issues, insecurity or intimidation). High functioning groups will often spend a few minutes actually identifying the criteria of distractions and brainstorming ways to set them aside.

So what is the clearest most incontrovertible evidence that a group is truly present and focused? Groups are present and focused when they are listening to each other. Without well-developed listening skills, no group will be able to enhance its collective intelligence. Listening and hearing are not the same things. Hearing tends to be passive, whereas listening requires attention and concentration.

We demonstrate our well-honed listening skills when we engage in collaborative inquiry; when we create what Laura Lipton and Bruce Wellman (2013) refer to as Communities of Thought. We demonstrate active listening when we pause and thoughtfully ponder a colleague's comment, paraphrase and probe for greater clarity.

What we say is also very important, but the ways in which we speak to each other may be even more so. The premise of this chapter is that the manner in which we conduct professional conversations in schools directly influences how collectively intelligent we are. We have written earlier that conversation is the primary mechanism through which we define, question and transform our sense of professional reality – the values, beliefs and assumptions that influence our decision-making and behaviors. As such, conversation is much too important to be left to chance – although more often that is the case.

Two ways of talking

There tends to be two ways that educators talk to each other: discussion and dialogue (Garmston & Wellman, 1998); 'Teacher talk that takes a difference', Ed Leadership). Both are necessary and appropriate depending upon the intention of the group or committee. But both are very different in purpose and process. Let's take a moment to look at each.

The purpose of discussion is to make a decision. Group members come to the meeting with ideas about what an effective way forward might be and they advocate for that outcome. Discussion often engages healthy cognitive conflict in which ideas and issues are analyzed, consequences predicted, pitfalls anticipated and alternatives evaluated. In discussions we engage in advocacy.

Ideally, a group that is engaged in advocacy is also practicing the seven norms of collaboration and is engaged in active, reflective listening so that the advocacy does not degenerate into personalized conflict or acrimonious debate. However, discussion is only one way of conducting a professional conversation. There is also dialogue.

The purpose of dialogue is to generate greater clarity and understanding by the group about the issue, topic or dilemma. There is no outcome other than generating deeper collective understanding. This may be difficult for some more task- or product-oriented group members to accept, particularly if they are unfamiliar with the concept of dialogue.

We may hear them asking: "So what is the purpose of this meeting?" or "Where do we go from here? Shouldn't we have an action plan?" At the heart of dialogue is collective and mutual learning: the value of the conversation is the conversation. The way that we talk with each other in a dialogue is through inquiry, using the norms of collaboration, particularly the three Ps of emotional intelligence: pausing, paraphrasing and probing.

One of the most profound differences between dialogue and discussion is that discussion tends to be self-focused. I have *my* ideas and opinions and the question is how best *I* will advocate for them so that *I* can persuade others of their effectiveness. Dialogue, on the other hand, tends to be other-focused in the sense that it is about listening to the ideas of other people, paraphrasing for clarity and probing in order to come to a deeper collective understanding.

It is often very helpful for groups to explicitly identify the type of conversation it will engage in, because our intentions will determine our conversational behavior. We can ask: what is the purpose of this meeting? What is our intended outcome? Will this be a dialogue or will it be a discussion?

As a general rule, groups are wise to engage in dialogue before discussion. If we have developed a deep understanding of an issue, we are in a much better position to enter a discussion that will result in a sound decision.

In the first edition of their book *The Adaptive School: the Facilitation of Collaborative Groups,* Bob Garmston and Bruce Wellman (1999) listed one of the seven norms of collaboration as 'Balancing advocacy and inquiry'. In the second edition this had been changed to 'Putting inquiry at the center'. We were intrigued and wrote to Bob and Bruce about the change. The answer came that in the opinion of the authors many, perhaps even most, groups misunderstand, undervalue and underuse inquiry. The change had been to emphasize the power of structured inquiry as a professional tool.

Let's take a brief look at a school group that begins a dialogue but finds itself pressured into premature discussion and advocacy.

A Tower of Babel

It was a decidedly odd and temporary situation: everyone was in agreement! Teachers, administration, the board of directors, parents, and even Patrick, the Headmaster of the Malaysian International School, were united behind the decision to introduce a second language in the elementary school. It was one of those rare decisions that everyone gets behind and is actually energized and inspired by the new initiative.

However, the good feeling was short lived. The devil, as usual, was in the details. The obvious next question was: which language to introduce. There was no shortage of candidates: European parents advocated for French and German. Canadians pressed for French. A sizable group of American parents pulled for Spanish. At the same time, a significant group of locally-resident parents thought Mandarin would help their children in the future. One educator wrote a well-reasoned appeal to teach Latin as it would be a sound base for all the Romance languages. Another group advocated for Bahasa Malayu – the host country language.

The Board of Directors sent Patrick and his administrative team away to study the question and to return with a recommendation in two month's time. The administration took the question under advisement. They surveyed other international schools in Southeast Asia and debated the relative merits, both educationally and politically, for the various languages. After much discussion, the administration recommended that Bahasa Malayu be introduced.

Patrick knew that it would not be a popular choice. Despite the fact that Bahasa, the language of Malaysia and Indonesia, is the fourth largest language in the world, many – perhaps even most of the parents – would not see it as useful to their children's education. Most of the children at MIS were expatriates and would not continue the study of Bahasa after their stay in Malaysia came to an end. Patrick and the admin team also suspected that there might have been some linguistic chauvinism among the parents. Bahasa did not represent a language from a dominant culture or economic power and as such was not held in high esteem among many of the parents.

So, given the negative reception that they anticipated, why did the administration unanimously recommend Bahasa? The educational reasons were obvious. The children were in a country where they could actually use the language. There were relevance and immediate opportunities to practice it. The entire support staff of the school spoke Bahasa and the opportunities for field trips were many and varied. The elementary school already had a rich program of teaching Malaysian culture and the language would be a natural addition to it.

In addition, when children learn a second language they develop what is called a 'language facility', which is transferable to other languages learned at a later stage. So, even if children didn't continue with their study of Bahasa in middle or high school, the study would indeed support their future language learning.

The recommendation split the board of directors and caused a long and acrimonious debate. The chairman was perceived as being biased and this resulted in personalized conflict. Pausing, paraphrasing and probing were cast aside in favor of exchanges of passionate opinions that often reflected self-interest. There was a great deal of advocacy, but not much inquiry. There were a few members who could see the educational reasons for Bahasa, but also who felt that its study would be a waste of time for their children. The difficult discussion continued late into the evening and the members became tired, hungry and irritable.

Finally a board member suggested that since the parents were paying the tuition bill, they should have a voice in the decision. He suggested a survey of parents as to which language they would like to see taught. Patrick attempted to suggest that this might not be the best way forward but he was drowned out by the enthusiasm that coupled a way forward and a blessed relief from the present impasse.

The surveys were sent out the following week. Results were collected and tabulated. French and Spanish were in a dead-heat for number one space; Mandarin came in third and Bahasa a distant fourth. A smattering of other languages came in for mention, including Urdu, Tamil, Khmer and Vietnamese.

At the next board meeting, the issue was on the agenda once again. None of the members had much appetite for French and Mandarin was not seen as politically viable if the school did not offer Bahasa. Patrick again stated the case for Bahasa Malayu. A vote was taken and Spanish was adopted as the language to be taught in the elementary school. The vote was along national lines with the six members voting for Spanish being US citizens and the five voting for Bahasa being non-Americans. Bad feeling prevailed for some time. Not only were there winners and losers on the board, but there was also resentment amongst both parents and teachers.

When we analyze this case study, we see initial inquiry. The board and the administration dispassionately analyzed the merits of a proposal to introduce a second language in the elementary school and achieved consensus that this was indeed the direction that the school should go.

The inquiry was characterized by emotionally detached dialogue. Board members listened carefully and asked clarifying questions. Research was shared about language acquisition and data was disseminated about what other international schools in the region were doing. This led to unanimous agreement to introduce a second language in the elementary school.

The dialogue, however, prematurely morphed into discussion and advocacy as board members (all parents of children at the school) recognized their own vested interests and were unable, in this instance, to put them aside. The suggestion to put out a survey to the parents may have sounded very fair and reasonable to the exhausted board members, but it represented a democratic form of decision-making that in no way ensured critical thinking, inquiry and analysis, or a well thought-out decision. (Once you survey the parents on an issue like this, you are almost certainly bound to publish the survey results and then it is extremely difficult to go against a significant majority, however, unthinking or self-serving their responses may have been.)

On such a controversial topic, it may have been wise for the board to bring in a neutral facilitator who could have set the ground rules for dialogue and inquiry and not permitted premature advocacy.

Historical footnote: Spanish language instruction was implemented in the elementary school at MIS, but in the years that ensued the demographics on the board shifted and Mandarin and Bahasa were added. Today,

Spanish continues to be taught in very small and very expensive classes.

There are different assumptions that underlie dialogue and discussion. At the heart of advocacy is the notion that there is a right answer or at least a best or better answer and the critical thinking of the group can provide access to an enlightened final decision. This is, of course, a necessary process in any complex organization.

The assumption that underlies dialogue is the basic tenet of constructivism: that all knowledge is tentative, what we teach today as gospel truth may well become tomorrow's falsehood. Complex issues, such as those that surround teaching and learning, require deep analysis and a by-product of such inquiry is that cherished beliefs may become discredited.

The tentative nature of knowledge is easy to grasp in an historical sense. It is not difficult to understand how Copernicus and Galileo's discoveries changed our understanding of the solar system. It is much more difficult to entertain that what we presently hold as immutable truths may in fact be completely wrong. While the tentativeness of knowledge may make us uncomfortable, the humility and skepticism embodied in such inquiry are a necessary compliment to our search for temporary certainty.

Organizations that strive to enhance their collective intelligence need to pay attention to the pattern of dialogue and discussion within their work groups. This can often be facilitated by school leaders who are sensitive to the differences between informational and transformational learning. Leadership for adult transformational learning is about inquiry and the process of developing deep understanding. While there are obviously no pure types of leaders, we would suggest that inquiry-centered leadership probably comes closest to realizing the goal of enhancing organizational intelligence.

Inquiry centered leaders

David Perkins (2003) suggests that leaders of organizations need to provide for the 'whither and the why'. The whither is about direction: where are we going as an organization? What is the short term and long term plan? The why question has to do with motivation. What are the reasons for such a plan? What benefits will there be in such a project? Why are we doing this – and why are we doing it this way?

Perkins goes on to identify four different types of leaders who he refers to as Answer-Centered Leaders, Vision-Centered Leaders, Leaders-by-Leaving-Alone, and Inquiry-Centered leaders.

Answer-centered leaders provide answers to questions. This is a very common conception of leadership. Answer-centered leaders are often bright, ambitious and very experienced. They know a great deal and are eager to share their knowledge and experience. They say: "It's the job of leaders to solve problems and I have a solution for you." They will certainly address the whither question, but often offer little in terms of the why. They do little to motivate teachers. In fact, because they are often internally motivated, they assume that everyone else is as well. At best, answer-centered leaders are perceived as helpful and responsive; at worst they are paternal and infantilize their subordinates.

Vision-centered leaders provide for both the whither and why questions: they provide both direction and motivation but may exclude possibilities that are not consonant with their vision. They may also create dependency relationships. The vision-centered leader may be similar to the charismatic leader that Jim Collins (2001) writes about in his book *Good to Great* in that when the leader leaves the organization, the vision also departs. The vision-centered leader doesn't necessarily facilitate collective knowledge processing and therefore may not actually enhance organizational intelligence.

Leadership by leaving alone: Although somewhat counter-intuitive, leadership by leaving people alone has some aspects to recommend it. Benign neglect actually makes room for people to rise to the occasion, figuring out the whither and why as best they can. However, this is a risky leadership style that does nothing to support the complex challenge of collective knowledge processing. Organizational intelligence happens, if it does, as a matter of chance.

Inquiry-centered leadership: When handled well, inquiry-centered leadership facilitates the group's collective knowledge processing around both the whither and why questions. It also models what effective knowledge processing looks like. It has the power to both inform and inspire. Michael Fullan (2000) suggests that sustainable school improvement is not brought about by compliance, but through school leaders nurturing the enthusiasm and energy for implementation. Inquiry-centered leadership holds this potential.

Inquiry-centered leadership does several things. First, it transforms leadership from a noun – a static position from which an individual welds power and authority – into a verb – a process of communal interaction and learning (Lambert 1998).

Secondly, inquiry-centered leadership strives to build leadership capacity in others. We believe this may be the highest form of leadership. Building leadership capacity in others involves a process of developing individual and collective emotional intelligence – this is a process that we examined in the previous chapter.

Inquiry-centered leadership in action in Dhaka

Inquiry-based leadership was evident at the American International School of Dhaka when the elementary principal met with her grade five teachers. The subject of their collaborative inquiry was how student peer assessment might enhance the learning of *both* the assessor and the student being assessed.

The previous assumption that been that the sole beneficiary of peer assessment was the student receiving the feedback. However, now the grade five team was wondering about the learning of the student doing the assessing. In what ways might the formation of constructive feedback enhance the learning of the student assessor?

The conversation focused on how the student assessor would use a rubric. One teacher suggested that the student assessors might find it easier if the rubric were translated into a series of questions. Another agreed and volunteered to draft out such questions. There was then a long pause. Finally, the principal asked what learning might be involved if the student assessors crafted the questions themselves. There was another long silence.

One teacher questioned whether the students would be able to do so. Good questions, she commented, take a lot of thought. Another expressed concern that teacher-generated questions might turn the assessment into a 'canned' activity. The other teachers agreed and suggested that the cognition required in framing good questions could involve important learning for the student assessors.

While still uncertain that fifth graders would be up to the task, the team of teachers and the principal set about devising a collective student activity that would include teacher support for the translation of the rubric into student-generated questions. This was a conversation that mattered, an example of inquiry based leadership.

Inquiry-centered leadership nurtures the five components of what Seashore-Louis, Marks & Kruse (1995) and Dufour & Eakin (1998) refer to as professional learning communities. These include shared norms and values, an unrelenting focus on student learning, collaboration, de-privatized practice and reflective dialogue. Let's examine each briefly.

Shared norms and values are the bedrock of our individual and collective professional identity. Values are truths that resonate within us at the deepest level. Values are not the same as strategies although they are often confused as such. A deeply-held value might be that all children need to be encouraged to do their best. Praising a child's efforts is a possible strategy for accomplishing this, but praise is not in and of itself a value. There are teachers who use praise very sparingly but nevertheless manage to encourage, inspire and motivate students.

Values motivate us and form the fabric of our mission as educators. One way in which organizations or groups can become more collectively intelligent is to explicitly identify and return to shared values. This builds group cohesion (we stand for something meaningful that is larger than ourselves) and is highly motivating. School leaders who recruit new teachers to a school philosophy or set of values (as opposed to working conditions or salary) have considerably higher retention rates.

Norms are not the same as values. Norms are behaviors that reflect values that are repeated so often that they become habitual – they represent the way things are done at his school. Norms reflect the deeply held values in action and are the observable manifestation of school culture.

A value for a particular school or task force might be open and honest dialogue. A norm that reflects this value might be honoring or embracing the resistance. Instead of dismissing or attempting to overpower the 'nay sayer', the group might welcome 'the devil's advocate' or 'critical friend' as an opportunity to further clarify issues and perhaps uncover unintended consequences. Norms operationalize values.

A focus on student learning is the proverbial touchstone. It seems a truism to state that student learning should be addressed daily and should form the centerpiece of the conversations that we have with colleagues and teachers. However, all too often student learning is lost in the labyrinth of issues that confront us daily.

Let's look at two contrasting examples, both that focus on the integration of educational technology. In a recent conversation with a teacher from New York City, we learned that several years ago interactive white boards had been installed in every classroom in his building.

The faculty had been given an introductory workshop by the manufacturer's representative as to what the so-called smart board could do, but no one had explicitly connected the new technology with student learning. No one had addressed the question of how the interactive white board could generate higher-order thinking or encourage effective communication. As a result, our colleague from New York reported that a year after installation most of the interactive white boards remained either unused or served as expensive screens on which PowerPoints were projected.

We invite you to contrast a second parallel situation. The United World College of South East Asia in Singapore invited us to facilitate a three day technology-mentoring workshop. We would provide the background in mentoring and adult learning and the tech. gurus at the UWC would provide the expertise in IT.

At the start of the workshop, the IT leadership stated the workshop premise very clearly: technology is here to support student learning. That was the critical connection and the workshop didn't deviate from it. The statement was revisited almost hourly over the next three days. There was a constant questioning of how a specific computer application might enhance student literacy or numeracy. What concepts might be more effectively introduced using a certain program? How might another application encourage student metacognition? As a result, there was a consistent focus on student learning and the transfer to the classroom of the skills learned in the workshop was greatly enhanced.

Collaboration takes place when members of a learning community work together as equals (irrespective of positions of authority) towards a common goal. Bob Garmston and Bruce Wellman (2009) write that 'collaboration is the norm in high performing and improving schools and results in increased student achievement ... However, collaboration skills need to be taught explicitly.'

There is a fairly common misconception that adults know intuitively how to work together as a team or group. A few people do seem to have a natural talent for social sensitivity and tend to instinctively gravitate towards effective collaborative behavior. However, research and experience suggests to us that most people do not do so. In our experience, deep collective inquiry that results in transformational adult learning and improved student learning within the classroom will not happen unless the group members have undergone specific training in collaboration.

In the previous chapter, we introduced the seven norms of collaboration. These represent both declarative and procedural challenges. One must understand what each means, the values that support them and how the norm might contribute to effective group information processing. But understanding the norms is insufficient. One must also practice them in a group setting, periodically self-assess against a norms inventory, and then set challenging individual and group goals.

When Bill was the headmaster at International School of Kuala Lumpur, he had a weekly meeting with the administrative team. About once every six weeks or so, the final ten minutes of the meeting would be given over to an evaluation of the group's effectiveness based on the norms of collaboration. The group would then decide which of the norms to pay close attention to over the next month or so.

Time and time again we have seen schools embrace the idea of collaboration but fail to provide either the time or training for it. This is a recipe for teacher frustration and ultimately, cynicism.

De-privatized practice takes place when teachers visit each other's classrooms and observe each other in the act of facilitating learning. This is such an obviously powerful and inexpensive form of professional learning, it is astounding that its practice is not more widespread!

In other professions, observation is a normal and expected procedure. We have only to think of the master surgeon making his rounds in a hospital with a train of medical students following, watching carefully the process of diagnosis. We have only to visit the law courts and witness the rows of law students listening to a master advocate argue a complex case. Why is peer observation so infrequently practiced in education? Historically, the adult-to-adult isolation of the teaching profession may be its greatest hubris.

We believe that there are two conditions that serve to inhibit teacher peer observation. One is emotional and one is organizational. In our experience having a colleague observe a lesson may produce anxiety for the teacher being observed. The observed teacher may be concerned about the evaluation and judgments that the observer may be making.

Less has been written about the anxiety experienced by the observer who frequently is unclear about what is to be observed, how the observation should be conducted and what is expected in terms of feedback. We believe that the mutual anxiety of the observed and the observer may greatly inhibit de-privatized teaching practice.

This anxiety is often generated out of a lack of clarity in three areas: a lack of clarity in the purpose of the peer observation (Why are we doing this?); a lack of clarity in the structure of the observation (Who determines what is observed? How does the observation actually take place? Are there dos and don'ts when visiting another teacher's classroom?); and a lack of clarity in the outcome (What is expected in a reflecting conversation? Does the observer provide feedback? If so, is the feedback evaluative or descriptive? What's the difference? What is the role of data?).

Without clarity in these areas we can expect both observed and the observer to practice avoidance tactics.

At the end of this chapter we have included a description of what we call a Protocol for the Rounds, a procedure that makes some practical suggestions for implementing a relatively anxiety-free program of peer observation that has clarity of purpose, structure and outcome. It has been implemented in a number of international schools and has been shown to enhance significantly organizational intelligence.

Reflective dialogue lies at the heart of all adult learning. From Plato to Solzhenitsyn, writers have suggested that, as a species, humans do not learn from experience. We only learn from *reflection upon experience*. There is an important distinction here. Here is the difference between a teacher who has taught for 20 years and a teacher who has taught for one year 20 times over.

Like 'collaboration', the word 'reflection' has been overused in educational circles to the point where it has either lost its meaning or it conjures up frustration and irritation on the part of the teachers (and students) hearing it. We visited one school in the Far East that prided itself on engaging students in reflecting on their own learning. In a conversation with a high school student, we asked how the reflective process was doing. The student replied: "I'm going to puke if I have to do any more reflecting." Although teachers may be more circumspect, their reactions may be similar.

We suspect that this negative response may be because we exhort teachers and students to reflect, but fail to provide a structure for it. There are few things as frustrating and stressful as being expected to engage in a process or activity without knowing how to do so. What does it mean to reflect? What does a reflective dialogue actually look like?

Genuine reflection is about personalized learning. It is a form of intellectual risk-taking in which the self-directed teachers (or student) undertakes self-assessment and then explores the factors that contributed to the outcome. Reflection can be a solitary activity, but this requires considerable self-discipline, maturity and introspection. It is unusual for solitary reflection to be meaningful without significant training. More commonly, we see transformational reflection taking place in coaching relationships either between two colleagues or in a small group.

Just as we cannot compel other people to learn, we cannot force teachers into reflection. We can create the conditions and set expectations, but we cannot mandate transformational learning because genuine reflection is self-directed. It can be supported by trusted colleagues and administrators, but the impetus comes from the individual concerned.

Costa and Garmston (2002) identify, as part of Cognitive Coaching[sm] a five-step process for reflective dialogue. The steps in the Reflecting Conversation Map support the person being coached in developing new insights and learnings and committing them to application. The steps include:

Asking the coachee to summarize his or her impressions of the lesson.

Asking the coachee to analyze the causal factors.

Supporting the coachee in developing new learning.

Having the coachee commit the new learning to application.

Inviting the coachee to reflect on the coaching conversation.

Journal writing is an effective way to begin a reflective dialogue as written expression permits an editing process that allows the individual to achieve greater precision with thought and language.

Research in the business sector is now confirming what our grandparents knew intuitively: that positive, curious and other-centered individuals are not only a pleasure to work with but can also contribute to highly productive work teams. Losada and Heaphy (2004) conducted a research study in over 60 business teams, examining how the emotional content of team conversation was correlated to productivity and effectiveness.

The researchers identified three areas of communication: positive and negative comments; the presence of inquiry and advocacy; and whether the conversation focused on self or others. The various teams were evaluated as high, medium or low based upon sales figures, customer satisfaction, and evaluations from supervisors. Conversational comments were judged to be positive if they were supportive (encouraging or appreciative) and negative if there were disapproving or sarcastic.

The results of their research are:

Conversational components in high, medium, and low performing teams

Performance Levels of Teams	Ratio of Positive to Negative Comments	Ratio of Presence of Inquiry to Advocacy	Ratio of Conversational focus on self as opposed to others
High	5:1	1:1	1:1
Medium	2:1	2:3	2:3
Low	1:3	1:19	1:29

If we define collective intelligence as group effectiveness, Losada and Heaphy's study suggests a powerful correlation between how we engage in conversation and the performance of the work team. Teams that had positive presuppositions that focused on inquiry were significantly more intelligent and effective.

Furthermore in another similar study, Losada found (Fredrickson and Losada, 2005) that work teams 'flourish' when the ratio of positive to negative comments is above 2.9 (the so-called *Losada Line*). They defined 'flourish' as teams that were adaptive, stable and highly innovative.

However, the authors caution that artificial, forced or disingenuous positivity will inevitably be interpreted as negativity. The study suggests that the point of diminishing returns was when the ratio of positive to negative comments reached above 11.

Benchmarking and inquiry

Over the last dozen years or so, schools have increasingly looked to benchmark themselves against other similar schools. This has produced some mixed and controversial results. At its best, benchmarking can produce rich, collaborative conversations that analyze data, identify innovation, share best practice and improve student learning. At its worst, it can result in reductionist thinking, insidious comparisons that produce so-called public league tables.

These rankings of schools are often associated with coercive measures. Schools that do well are financially rewarded; those that do less well are financially punished. These coercive measures, coupled with an emphasis on 'making your numbers', have led more than just a few school districts to engage in professional deceit and dishonesty. How do we ensure that benchmarking contributes to enhanced collective intelligence?

To start with, we need to be absolutely clear about our intentions and then choose congruent behaviors, which sounds simple but in practice in is complex and challenging. Let's examine an example of benchmarking that worked particularly well.

For six years, Bill served as headmaster of the International School of Kuala Lumpur (ISKL) in Malaysia. ISKL was a member of the Interscholastic Association of Southeast Asian Schools (IASAS), a group of six, large, high functioning international schools in Southeast Asia.

Each September the six heads of school would gather for a weekend retreat to 'benchmark' the six schools. Prior to the weekend retreat, data would be gathered in easily quantifiable areas such as student enrollment, teacher-student ratios, class size, budget cost centers, and standardized test scores. However, data was also gathered in other areas that were less easy to quantify, such as teacher supervision practices, professional learning initiatives, curriculum design and mapping, and community building.

At the start of each annual retreat, the intention of the benchmarking was explicitly stated: the exercise was to inquire into what our respective schools were doing in terms of innovative practice; how common problems and issues were being addressed; and to share best (or 'better') practice. The norms of interaction included round robin mini-presentations that were punctuated with paraphrasing and probing questions.

The purpose of the retreat was to be mutually supportive, not to engage in competition. There was an implicit understanding that the pursuit of excellence was not a mutually exclusive activity. ('You do not need to fail in order for me to succeed.')

In addition, there was a mutual agreement that the data shared and the content of the conversations would be confidential – even from the respective boards of directors. The potential for the misuse of information was ever present. Both trust and respect were present in these meetings and Bill reports they were some of the richest and most meaningful professional conversations he has engaged in.

Collaborative inquiry and innovation

Keith Sawyer (2007) argues persuasively that creativity is almost always a collaborative process that masks itself in the romance of the lone genius having a breakthrough in his garage. He further suggests that creativity emerges from the way in which we work together. Sawyer states that innovation emerges over time with high performing teams demonstrating deep listening; group members building on each other's ideas and tolerating uncertainty, ambiguity and the temporary absence of meaning. In such an atmosphere surprising questions surface. The most creative groups are better at finding new problems than solving old ones (Sawyer, 2007).

Genuine innovation is not often associated with schools because many, perhaps even most, school cultures are conservative and risk-adverse. However, there are other factors in schools that also serve to inhibit productive discourse that fosters innovation in other fields of endeavor.

Wellman (2013) suggests that there are three major constraints to productive discourse: cognitive constraints, affiliative constraints, and ego-centric constraints. Cognitive constraints have to do with not having the necessary information or expertise which can produce 'self-sealing logic' (*eg* confusing experience for expertise). Smart groups are aware when they have reached the frontiers of their knowledge and expertise and then actively look outward, particularly seeking information that may conflict with their assumptions. Self-sealing logic is a close relative to Collins's (2001) silo-thinking – the inability or unwillingness to look beyond one's one silo and make meaningful connections.

Affiliative constraints have to do with the difficulties that group members may encounter when navigating task and relational tension. Inquiry into sensitive or controversial issues can be hampered by both friendships and adversarial relationships with the group.

Ego-centric constraints develop when one or more group members demonstrate a need for control or dominance or low regard for other members of the group or the collective group process. Such need for control is often fear-based and we hear it when individuals announce that they don't trust collective thought.

One of the reasons that innovation is absent in most schools is that innovation is inefficient. If groups are going to be truly creative, they must fail frequently. Schools have an extremely low tolerance for failure. Sawyer (2007) quotes Intel Director Mary Murphy-Hoye as proclaiming: "If we're not failing ten times more than we are succeeding, it means we are not taking enough risks." (p109)

Sawyer's mantra on failure states: 'Fail often, fail early, and fail gloriously.' (p178) He is drawing a direct correlation between innovation and an organizational culture that accepts failures, recognizes them in their early stages (doesn't throw good money after bad) and appreciates the intrinsic value of our failures.

While no one is suggesting that schools should enter a risk-embracing contest with the technology giants, we might be wise to think a little about how our need for control, order and certainty might be inhibiting our organization's intelligence.

Innovation has a bad name in education. It is frequently dismissed by teachers as yet another fad, the so-called flavor of the month that someone in authority is trying to impose. However, we would argue that some school-based innovations have incredible staying power. They are not fads, but rather powerful strides that our profession has taken to enhance learning.

Some examples include cooperative learning groups, experiential learning, constructivism, differentiation, metacognition and the current emphasis on providing meaningful formative assessment. So what distinguishes a temporary fad from a lasting innovative breakthrough? We suggest that the distinction emerges in collaborative critical inquiry when we subject new ideas to the scrutiny of the groups.

However, we know that simply putting people into groups doesn't insure creativity, productivity or meaningful critical inquiry. For collaborative inquiry to be meaningful and innovative the following guidelines are useful:

Don't use groups for tasks that can be better performed by individuals. For example, don't write a report by committee. Send an individual away to write a draft and then review it by committee.

Make sure the group goal is clear and that there are specific success indicators.

Make active listening the norm (pause, paraphrase, probe).

Use tools, structures and protocols that promote collaborative inquiry. (Arguably the greatest waste of time in organizations such as schools is the assumption that groups will know how to organize collective work naturally – without the use of specific protocols or skillful facilitation).

Employ the norms of collaboration; look for constructive patterns. Patterns become habits, habits become norms, norms influence behavior.

Self-assessment and descriptive feedback drive group growth.

Manage the paradox of blending autonomous individuals and group consciousness.

Keep groups to the minimum number of team members required.

Use a skilled facilitator.

Allow for frequent breaks.

Ensure equal participation.

Collaborative inquiry can be transforming and re-vitalizing. For example, in the early days of the French Impressionist movement in art, rejection, mockery and scorn were the most common reactions of the *grand salons*. Claude Monet wrote of his conversations with his fellow artists (Pissaro, Degas, Cezanne, Renoir, and Sisley):

> Your mind was held in suspense all the time, you spurred the others on to sincere, disinterested inquiry and were spurred on yourself, you laid in a stock of enthusiasm that kept you going for weeks on end until you could give final form to the idea you had in mind. You always went home afterwards better steeled for the fray, with a new sense of purpose and a clearer head. (in Sawyer, 2007, p. 133)

Collaborative inquiry across cultures

International schools are by definition composed of leaders, teachers, students and parents from many different cultures. What makes the international school experience both rich and challenging is that culture is often expressed implicitly and needs to be uncovered. Schein (in van der Heijden, 2002) defines culture as 'the total set of socially determined tacit assumptions that the group shares about how the world works but does not articulate to each other'. Geert Hofstede uses a computer metaphor to define culture as 'the collective programming of the mind, which distinguishes the members of one group or category of people from another' (in van der Heijden, p96).

In international schools there are multiple opportunities for cultural misunderstanding and the ever-present trap of making unsophisticated generalizations about the other culture. Increasingly international schools are recognizing that developing cross cultural competency is a core value of international mindedness or global citizenship – the capacity to move knowledgably and gracefully across and between cultures.

Collaborative inquiry is made both richer and more challenging when the members of the group or team come from different national or organizational cultures because differences in values affect decision making and behaviors within organizations. From Starbucks in the Forbidden City to McDonalds in France to Disney World in Paris, multi-national corporations provide a vivid tapestry of cultural conflicts that have emerged from value differences.

There are also cultural dimensions to our understanding of what it means to listen. Americans tend to think that it is the responsibility of the speaker to communicate clearly and that the listener shouldn't have to do any real work. But in other cultures (particularly those in Asia and Africa) that value indirect and metaphoric speech, creative listening is highly valued (Sawyer, 2007).

Bill once worked with a business manager from the Wachagga tribe from the north of Tanzania. She was chairing a meeting of the school's finance committee and was trying to get the members to appreciate the dangers and risks of using the school's strategic financial reserves to cover operational expenses. She explained that the school was "eating from its hump", something African cattle do during periods of famine and drought. The western members of the committee concluded that the business manager was a poor communicator.

In order to engage in collaborative inquiry, international schools need to explore cultural value differences. According to Geert Hofstede (in Van der Heijden, 2002), who researched cultural differences for IBM in more than 70 countries using more than 100,000 questionnaires, there are a number of significant areas that illustrate differences in values across difference cultures. These include: power distance, risk avoidance, individualism and collectivism and what Hostede referred to as masculine and feminine cultures.

Power distance is the separation in terms of influence and authority between two individuals as perceived by the less powerful. Some cultures have fairly rigid attitudes towards social hierarchies in which there is considerable inequality in power and authority. On the other hand, there are some cultures in which these attitudes are more flexible and egalitarian.

As a general rule collaborative inquiry and reflective dialogue require a degree of openness and honesty and there is greater likelihood of this being present in a society with low power distance. That said, there are hierarchical societies that have found ways to manage the need for collaborative critical thinking and high power distance. It is common in Japan, for instance, for disagreements to take place informally behind closed doors and when the formal meeting takes place 'agreed minutes' have already been prepared.

Sometimes we are asked whether it is possible to teach collaboration skills in a traditional, hierarchical culture. Our answer is a resounding 'yes'. We have successfully taught the skills of professional collaboration to schools in Indonesia, India, China, and various countries in Africa and South America. However, the cultural values need to be uncovered, and norms established, so that the newly-acquired collaborative behaviors are not misinterpreted as discourteous or lacking in respect.

Risk avoidance is the degree to which cultural groups tend to feel comfortable with uncertainty. In cultures where risk avoidance is high we see an emphasis on job security and continuity, adherence to rules and regulations and a low tolerance for ambiguity. A number of western European countries exhibit high risk avoidance in that their populations are willing to trade very high taxation rates for security in terms of health care, unemployment benefits and pensions.

On the other hand, in low risk avoidance cultures there is a greater willingness to take risks and a lower level of resistance to change. In our experience, schools (irrespective of where they are located) share with organized religion the tendency to be high-risk avoidance organizations.

Individualism and collectivism have to do with whether the primary focus of the culture is centered upon self-determination or whether individuals subordinate self-interest to the greater good of the group. In societies that celebrate the rugged individual, there tends to be looser ties between individuals. Family constellations are smaller and more fragile, and there is arguably a greater degree of loneliness and alienation – particularly in old age. Collectivist societies place greater value on the extended family and have clear expectations that individuals are to subjugate self-interest to the welfare of the larger group.

Generally, school teachers tend towards relationship orientation. The fact that they choose a service oriented profession such as teaching in the first place suggests that in most cases schools will have more of a collectivist than individualist orientation. This is, of course, a generalization, but it has been borne out in the thousands of hours that we have spent trying to explain the culture of international schools to ruggedly individualistic board members who have great difficulty understanding why bonuses and individual merit pay simply won't work in schools.

Masculine and feminine cultures are defined by Hofstede in terms of the traditional gender stereotypes. Masculine cultures are characterized by the acquisition of material possessions; the accumulation of power, position, influence and reputation; and individual achievement. Feminine cultures are characterized by relationship development, concern for others, and interdependence; they tend to be less aggressive and competitive and there is markedly less role differentiation between genders: both men and women work in the same jobs.

As a general rule schools tend to have relatively low power distance, high risk avoidance, and a collectivist and feminine culture making them almost incomprehensible to rugged individualistic male board members or politicians. It is no wonder that so many externally mandated 'school improvement initiatives' have been miserable failures.

'Wicked' problems and oscillating systems

Occasionally schools will face truly wicked problems that defy all efforts at traditional, linear problem-solving processes. Often these wicked problems are recursive because they represent oscillating systems. An oscillating system is a sophisticated form of collective stupidity. It results when a problem produces a solution that returns the school or teacher to either the original problem or even a more severe variation thereof.

A simple example might be when Bill goes on holiday to France and indulges in cheeses, pates, *crème brulé* and, of course, wines. He returns at the end of the holiday several kilos heavier than at its start. The problem is being overweight; therefore, the solution is obviously a diet. Bill goes on a diet, but finds that dieting is a depressing exercise. And when Bill gets depressed he nibbles. He nibbles on popcorn, and cookies, ice cream and cake. In short, the dietary solution to Bill's problem has brought him back to the original problem – gaining unwanted kilos. Such is the nature of an oscillating system.

It is often impossible for schools to problem-solve their way out of an oscillating system. The symptoms of the problem often become confused with the cause; traditional linear problem-solving techniques fail to produce meaningful outcomes and can lead to circular arguments and widespread frustration. There are also times in which truly wicked problems don't call for solutions but rather for polarity management.

Polarity management is the handling of persistent, chronic issues that are unavoidable and unsolvable (Johnson 1996). For example, the ever-present tension between the high school principal who wants to spend money on the latest and most effective educational resources and the business manager who is determined to conserve resources and stay within the budget. The Center for Adaptive Schools has some extremely useful material for mapping and managing polarities.

To emerge from an oscillating system, the organization needs to become more collectively intelligent. It needs, in Michael Fullan's (2000) words, to engage in a 'ruthless re-examination of reality'. This is often a difficult and painful process and many times involves distinguishing between technical and adaptive challenges.

Technical and adaptive challenges

Generally speaking there are two types of challenges that organizations face: technical and adaptive. Technical challenges can be solved by informational learning. For example, if I purchase a new software package and I don't know to use it, I can read the instruction manual or take an online tutorial course: the challenge is technical, the solution is informational learning that results in changes in our behavior or enhancement in our capabilities.

Technical challenges are relatively easy to address if we have the appropriate resources. If we can solve a problem with a technical solution we should certainly do so – this is the easiest and most energy efficient way to approach such a problem. However not all challenges are technical.

Adaptive challenges are more complex. They involve changes to our internal self: modifications to our values, our beliefs, and even at times our identity. This is true at an individual and collective level. Adaptive challenges require experimentation, new discoveries, and adjustments that are both internal and external to self.

Heifetz & Linksy (2002) write: 'Without learning new ways – changing attitudes, values and behaviors – people cannot make the adaptive leap necessary to thrive in the new environment.' (p13) In short, adaptive challenges require transformational learning. This is true for individuals and for organizations. Fullan (2011) suggests that adaptive challenges are 'adaptive' because they involve social complexity.

Technical and adaptive challenges

Challenge	What Needs Modification	Type of Learning Required
Technical Challenge	Behaviors and capabilities	Informational learning
Adaptive Challenge	Values, beliefs, and identity	Transformational Learning

There is a common misconception that we can address an adaptive challenge with a technical solution. The mismatch is extremely common and when the failure becomes evident, as it almost always does, it results in huge resistance to change, frustration and cynicism. When we attempt to address an adaptive challenge with a technical solution we may inadvertently create a vicious oscillating system.

We hear oscillating systems when...

Our goal is...	The immediate response is...	The secondary response is...
To develop greater differentiation	"Yes, but..."	"Where will the time come from?"
To improve teacher collaboration	"Yes, but..."	"The teachers will feel threatened..."

In each of the cases above, the goal appears to warrant a technical solution. If our desired outcome is greater differentiation, let's provide professional development, bring in a consultant, schedule a workshop, and have the teachers form a book study group. These activities will certainly provide informational learning. The assumption is that all teachers need are a few more instructional strategies. Informational learning should do the trick...

However, the secondary responses above suggest that we may be dealing with an adaptive challenge. Behind the question: "Where will the time come from?" may be the concern that if I try something new and challenging in the classroom, my instructional pedagogy may not be as effective. What I'm doing now seems to be working; why are you making me change? Not only do I have the students' learning to be concerned about, but also my own professional self-esteem. I take pride in my work. I don't want to be a second rate teacher. No amount of informational learning will address the adaptive challenge that this teacher is facing.

An oscillating system is by definition self-defeating. It defines a problem superficially and proposes a technical solution that in many cases becomes a larger problem than the original one was. Arguably the most prevalent oscillating system in education is the one facing the United States. Over the last two decades 'the problem' has been identified as poor standardized test results resulting from mediocre instruction. Rarely do we see such sweeping generalizations given such credence. The solution, then, to mediocre instruction must be *accountability* with some teeth in it.

Unfortunately the teeth are false. The extrinsic rewards and punishments that we inflict on individuals and schools are disrespectful and actually atrophy intrinsic motivation. The supposed solution exacerbates the problem.

We are only beginning to see the damage that oscillating systems can create. A more thoughtful approach was taken by Mourshed, Chinezi, & Barder in the so-called McKinsey Report (2010) where they stress that schools need improvement interventions that are appropriate to their developmental status – *balancing accountability interventions with capacity building.*

What makes oscillating systems so difficult to deal with is that the 'ruthless re-examination of reality' often requires us to re-evaluate our own cherished beliefs and values. Harvard Professor Robert Kegan (2009) suggests that each of us has an immunity to change system that operates both individually and collectively. These systems are self and group protective in that they insure the preservation of the *status quo.* This is even when the *status quo* is not working well, producing undesirable results, is counterproductive and self-defeating, and/or generating a toxic school culture.

Kegan (2009) suggests that one way to approach the ruthless re-examination of reality is to engage in 'immunity to change mapping'.

Since the immunity to change mapping process often involves deep transformational learning, it is best undertaken with a trained coach. The first step is to support the individual to identify the one big issue they wish to address.

This is a crucial stage since, if the goal is either unclear or insignificant, the remainder of the map will either be meaningless or trivial. The coach needs to hold the coachee at this step until a clear and robust goal(s) emerges. The next step is to have the coachee identify the visible commitments to the *status quo.* In other words, the coachee describes the behaviors that he or she wishes to change and the surface-level rationale for them.

In the third step, the coachee identifies what Kegan calls the 'Hidden Commitment to the Status Quo'; these reflect the values and beliefs that motivate the undesirable behavior. The final step is to identify the big assumption(s) upon which the values and beliefs are predicated. When skillfully applied, the four steps of immunity to change mapping takes the individual from the existing state to a vision of the desired states by way of a gradual exploration of behaviors and capabilities, the values and beliefs upon which they are based and finally to some assumptions and questions about identity.

The example below comes from Myles, the chairman of the high school social studies department in a large international school in Europe. Myles had identified that while his department was convivial and that relationships were positive and pleasant, the department was not making the kind of progress that he would have liked in unit planning and curriculum mapping.

Myles wanted to explore the relationship between his leadership of the department and its lack of productivity. Myles worked with a trained coach who supported his reflection at each step of the process. The map that follows below was the product of six months work.

Goal Statement (The one big thing…)	Visible Commitment to the Status Quo	Hidden Commitment to the Status Quo	Big Assumption(s): the immunity to change
To provide leadership that helps my department become more productive… To be more task-oriented… To be more assertive and directive… To learn how to say "NO" to tasks that aren't my responsibility…	I practice a very democratic style of meeting management. People often get off topic. I have trouble delegating tasks and holding people accountable for deadlines. I feel uncomfortable telling people what to do. I often take on other people's work when I don't think they will finish it.	I don't want to appear authoritarian or dictatorial. I'm uncomfortable being the 'bad guy'. I need to be needed by colleagues. I want to be one of the 'guys'. Members of my team won't like me if I hold them accountable.	I assume that if I provide direction and structure for my department, I will be disliked and ostracized. I assume that other people do not share my sense of responsibility. I assume that my current perception of team leadership is the only one that will work for me. I wonder if my willingness to take on other's people's tasks is contributing to group irresponsibility.

The above example of immunity to change mapping is individual, but the process can be used with a group. In both cases a trained coach or facilitator is advisable. When working with a less than effective group a powerful strategy can be an Assumption Wall (please see the Guided study questions, activities and case studies at the end of this chapter) that, in a similar fashion, serves to surface assumptions that may be standing in the way of enhanced collective intelligence.

Guided study questions

The authors contend that group intelligence is often reflected in the quality of our conversations. Think back to a particularly meaningful or stimulating conversation that you participated in. What made it so? What were the conditions under which it took place? What are you learning about high quality conversations?

Dialogue and discussion are both necessary in schools. However, the authors stress that dialogue and inquiry should be the centerpieces of our conversations. In what ways does dialogue enhance organizational intelligence and what opportunities do you have for promoting dialogue in your school?

In what ways can school leadership promote a culture of inquiry?

What are some oscillating systems that may be operating within your school? How do you go about identifying adaptive challenges and how do you deal with them?

In what ways might immunity to change mapping be useful to you individually or to your team or school?

Micro-teaching – a protocol for the rounds

John Hattie (2009), in his book *Visible Learning*, has conducted an exhaustive meta-analysis of over 800 research studies on the various influences on student learning. In the final analysis, Hattie ranks over a 135 influences on student learning on the basis of their effect size.

Micro-teaching as a professional learning activity ranks in the top ten. The description of the activity that follows combines the analysis of micro-teaching with a protocol for walk-through observations. It was developed at the International School of Kuala Lumpur by Susan Napoliello and Bill Powell. {For a more in depth look at this protocol, please see Powell, W. & Napoliello, S. (2005) 'Using Observation to Improve Instruction', *Educational Leadership*, Feb. 2005, p52-55.}

This process encourages enhanced instructional pedagogy through reflective dialogue. The outcome of the protocol is a structured conversation that is focused on an inquiry into effective teaching and learning.

Each 'walk through observation', including the follow-up meeting with the teachers who were observed, should take no more than about 75 minutes. The observations are entirely non-judgmental (no criticism/ no praise). There are no commendations and no recommendations. No advice is given. Both the observing team and the teachers being observed are volunteers who understand the purpose and structure of the protocol.

Structure of protocol

The team of observers meets for a briefing (ten minutes). Observer teams should be composed of both administrators and teachers. Teams should be limited to no more than four persons. Walk through observations should take no more than five minutes in each classroom. The number of classrooms being observed should be limited to four. Observers look for instructional practices that promote student learning. No note taking or clipboards.

Observers meet to discuss what they have observed. They make a list of instructional practices that promote student learning (not specifying which classroom they were observed in) and analyze (not evaluate) what they have observed. The observing team then frames a reflective question. The list of instructional strategies and the reflective question are then emailed to the teachers who were observed.

The observing team and the teachers who were observed meet for a conversation (20-25 minutes) that focuses on the reflective question. A facilitator needs to be identified who will keep the conversation on track by pausing, paraphrasing and probing. The conversation should take place either on the same day as the observation or the following day.

Examples of some reflective questions that were used at the International School of Kuala Lumpur to generate reflective dialogue included:

Pre-school: "What are some things you look for as evidence that a student is in his or her zone of proximal development while the student is engaged in self-directed play?"

Grade four: "What strategies do you use to sustain the cognitive engagement of all students while providing wait time for a specific child?"

Grade eight humanities: "Knowing that optimal learning takes place when there is both psychological safety and maximum challenge, in what ways do you architect these conditions and how do you manage to balance them?"

Structured reflective inquiry (knowing our students)

One characteristic of enhanced organizational intelligence is when teachers individually and collectively strive to know their students at deep levels as learners. We have developed a conversation map that focuses on knowing a specific student.

This inquiry often produces a rich learner profile. We have also found that by coming to know one child, the teacher is better able to understand clusters of children who may have similar characteristics. The conversation can take place in pairs or a group can form a 'fish bowl' around the coach and coachee and then debrief on the process afterwards.

Instructions to the coach/facilitator

Ask the coachee to identify a current student who interests him or her for whatever reason.

Ask the coachee to talk about why the student interests him/her.

Coach/facilitator expresses empathy (paraphrase the emotion).

Coach/facilitator paraphrases the content.

Coach probes for specificity about the student's interests. (If this student were to design a field trip, what might the location be?)

Coach probes for the child's strengths. (When have you seen the student doing his/her best work? In what media have you seen him/her produce his/her best work?)

Summarize the child's strengths.

Coach asks how the teacher is incorporating those strengths and interests into unit planning.

Coach asks the teacher what he or she is learning from the student

Coach invites coachee to reflect on the conversation. (In what ways has this conversation been useful to you?)

Note: Depending on the direction the inquiry takes, the coach might choose to probe into areas such as how the teacher's attitudes and expectations might be influencing student learning or something that the teacher might change or do differently.

Activity: assumption wall

Assumptions are critically important as they are powerful influences on our behavior and decision-making, and most are held at a subconscious, or at least unexamined level. The assumption wall is an activity that brings to the surface assumptions and allows us to examine and analyze them and explore their implications.

The facilitator announces the topic of the inquiry. It could be a school-wide goal or some aspect of the school that is under examination (*eg* unit planning, student behavior, teacher evaluation *etc*). The assumption wall activity works best with relatively small groups of, say, six to ten participants. If you have a larger group, break them into table groups of five or six.

First, each participant writes down a series of assumptions that he or she may have about the topic. The topic can be framed in the form of a provocative newspaper headline (for instance 'Teacher evaluation is inconsistent'. Or 'Unit planning in the IB Diploma programme is a waste of time').

Each participant is given a sticky note or a strip of paper and asked to write briefly (no more that 12 to 15 words) an assumption that he or she holds about the topic. This strip is then posted anonymously on an 'assumption wall'. The facilitator then models the inquiry by asking reflective questions and paraphrasing the participants' comments. With skilful facilitation (avoiding anything that sounds like interrogation) a rich reflective dialogue can ensue.

The Final Word: reading protocol

The Final Word is a reading protocol that generates a highly structured reflective inquiry. It operates as follows:

Participants have individually read a piece of text and have highlighted what they consider to be key or interesting ideas.

In groups of five or six, participants number off.

Person one shares a sentence or two that he or she has highlighted but makes no other comment.

Person two comments on person one's selection and then person three does the same. This continues round robin until all table group members have had a chance to comment.

After having the benefit of listening to all the other comments, Person one has the final word.

There is no cross talk.

The pattern is repeated until time is called.

Facilitator note: Because the instructions are complex, it is a good idea to check for understanding by asking a participant to paraphrase them.

Case study: making or inflating the grade

Augie Blanton waited patiently to bring up his problem. The other members of the administration might have heard about his issue, but he assumed that since it was a 'high school problem', they wouldn't be very interested. Augie was the high school principal.

There was a pause in the discussion and Lillian Rushworth, the director of the school, announced that it was time for Any Other Business.

Augie raised his hand.

"You may have heard that some of our parents are upset with the IB examination results…"

"I'm glad you're bringing this up. Last night at the Health Spa, Mrs Barrington…" Monika Chuggles inserted. Monika was the middle school principal.

"Please, let me finish, Monika." The intensity of Augie's voice increased, underscoring some of the stress he had been under lately. "There is a group of fairly upset parents. They're disappointed in their students' exam results and they're holding the school responsible. In two cases, kids haven't got into their first choice universities."

"What's the issue?" Lillian asked. She had been trained as a lawyer and had a fine analytic mind. Lillian could be counted on to cut to the chase.

"The parents are blaming the teachers, particularly in math and science."

"Are the teachers responsible?" Lillian demanded.

Augie paused and stroked his salt and pepper moustache. This was the moment of truth. "Yes," he began, "I think the teachers are responsible, but not exactly in the way the parents are suggesting. The parents are questioning teacher competency. I am their supervisor and I don't see anything wrong with their competency. I think this is a systems problem."

"A systems problem?"

"Yes. I think there is a clash between our internal system of grading and the IB's system of marking exams."

"Tell us more, Augie."

"I have reviewed the school's internal grades and the IB exam scores for students over the last three years and there is a consistent discrepancy. We are giving grades on our school report cards that are consistently higher than the actual IB scores."

"Our teachers are involved in grade inflation?" Lillian asked.

"You could put it that way. What has happened is that our internal grades have created unrealistic expectations in the minds of the parents and this has caused great disappointment when the actual exam results are released."

"Your recommendation?" Lillian asked, casting one eye to the watch on her left wrist.

"We need to bring our internal grading system into line with the IB."

"And since we have no control over the IB…"

"Our system will need to change."

"It seems, Augie, that you have identified both the problem and the solution. Well done. I appreciate school leaders that bring both problems and solutions to the table. It saves everyone a great deal of time." Lillian cast her eyes around the table at the other administrators. "Now, let's get to work on it so we don't have parents beating down our doors!"

Three months later, Augie sat alone in his office. It was Saturday morning and because there was no school, there was a temporary lull in the firestorm.

Following the admin meeting in August, Augie had put out a memo to the high school faculty explaining the discrepancy between the internal grades and the IB exam results and the resulting parental concern. He directed the faculty to the IB mark schemes and grade descriptors and asked everyone teaching IB courses to bring their grades into alignment with the IB standards.

Initially, there had not been much faculty reaction. Augie interpreted this as an indication that the teachers saw the reasonableness of his directive. However as the first marking period approached, Augie began to get emails from teachers asking for clarification. Then at the October faculty meeting there was a barrage of teacher questions. Augie was caught off guard and simply repeated his earlier instruction that internal grades needed to be aligned with the IB mark scheme.

On 24th October the high school report cards went home and for the next two days Augie's phone rang off the hook. The parents were up in arms about the grades. Straight A students were now getting Bs and Cs without any explanation. And more importantly, these grades were going on student's transcripts that would be used by prestigious American universities in their admissions decisions.

Lillian called Augie on the carpet. "What on earth have you done? Your new grading system has the parents up in arms. We have a virtual revolt on our hands."

Augie nodded reluctantly in agreement.

"Can I suggest," Lillian announced, "that we go back to the old system? At least then the problems were manageable?"

Augie thought about his own evaluation. Lillian didn't tend to inflate her grades, especially when they were connected to contract renewal. Augie nodded and mentally started to prepare a memo for his faculty.

Discussion questions

In what ways does this case study present an oscillating system?

What are the values and beliefs that reside at the heart of the issues?

Some problems cannot be 'solved', but can be managed. What is the difference between 'solving' and 'managing'? How might this problem have been managed more effectively?

Chapter 6

Organizational intelligence and the inclusion of students with special learning needs

"We choose to go to the moon. We choose to go to the moon in this decade and do the other things, not because they are easy, but because they are hard, because that goal will serve to organize and measure the best of our energies and skills, because that challenge is one that we are willing to accept, one we are unwilling to postpone, and one which we intend to win..."

President John F. Kennedy, 1962

Like President Kennedy, schools that embrace the journey towards including students with special learning needs do so not because it is easy, but because it is hard; because the goal will serve to organize and measure the best of our energies and skills; and because that challenge is one we are willing to accept, unwilling to postpone, and in which we intend to succeed.

In short, the thoughtful and planned inclusion of students with special needs will serve to enhance our collective intelligence. In this chapter, we will explore the relationship between rigorous challenges, group learning and growth of organizational intelligence. We will also examine how intelligent schools are sensitive to today's environment, monitoring and adapting to the changing student demographics in schools.

Whereas in previous decades, parents with children who had special learning needs were hesitant to take them abroad, parents today are expecting their children to be served and educated in international schools.

Finally, we will examine the benefits of collaborative interdependence between and among schools as we support the learning of children with special needs. Even if we don't have all the answers, our creativity, thoughtfulness and expertise are strengthened through our collaboration with others within the school and throughout the global community.

More than a decade into the 21st century, there are still many international school leaders (and thus, many international schools) who make decisions not to admit students with special learning needs. Some of the learning needs may involve mild to moderate learning disabilities or other developmental disabilities that make learning in traditional classrooms more challenging – for teachers as well as for students.

Some of the student applicants may also have severe learning needs, which do require intensive support. Ironically, to our knowledge, no child has ever been refused admission because s/he was too bright or intelligent for the school. Having said that, we know that truly gifted children are also often fragile learners and require learning support. Generally, children who have been and continue to be denied admission are those whose learning patterns and practices (or simply the lack of appropriate professional support) have resulted in poor academic reports.

Why we say "no" to children

When asked for the rationale behind their decision to deny admission to certain students, school leaders have given answers that include the following:

"Because we don't have to. We're a college preparatory school."

"We don't have a program for children with such learning needs."

"We can't be all things to all people."

"There are other schools that are better equipped to handle such students."

"If we accepted children like these, we might get a reputation for being a special needs school."

"The other international school in this city is the 'soft, fuzzy' option. We're the rigorous and academic school."

"We choose not to."

"It would be morally wrong to accept a child for whom we do not have a program."

For the expatriate parent, a school's decision not to admit their child(ren) may mean having to make a choice between a career and a child's education. Sometimes, schools have added insult to injury, by deciding that only some children from a single family – not all – are to be admitted, saying, "Well, we just don't have a program for your other child."

The resulting confusion and consternation on the parts of the parents are not hard to imagine. Our colleague, Kevin Bartlett from the International School of Brussels, asks questions that resonate: "What gives us the right to cherry pick which children, from which families, we might admit? What gives us the right to select only those who will provide us with the least challenge?"

Admittedly, the admission of any child with special learning needs requires thoughtful planning and careful consideration in all aspects of school life, not just the student's schedule of classes or assignment of teachers. We would want to review such an admissions case in light of the faculty's expertise and its *will to serve,* and the environment of welcome that might be extended to these students.

We would also want to make sure that student admissions in this area is *managed,* that we don't exceed our capacity to serve children well. In short, the inclusion of students with special learning needs requires a thoughtful re-examination of our identity as an educational organization.

We need to reflect on our collective purpose and mission. This is transformational learning that addresses a real and pressing adaptive challenge. If we're not yet where we want to be as an institution, how might we get there? What steps might we need to take to further realize our desired identity?

In other words, the thoughtful inclusion of students with special learning needs is one very practical and explicit way of enhancing a school's organizational intelligence. By challenging ourselves to do more than what we are already comfortable doing, we engage in a rigorous exercise of collaborative inquiry that supports our collective intellectual growth and social and emotional development. Taking the easy option isn't going to get us there.

Many years ago, when Bill began his tenure as headmaster at the International School of Kuala Lumpur (ISKL), a family applied for admission. Being responsible and prepared parents, they sent their children's applications and supporting documents well ahead of time. There was a stumbling block: Peter (not his real name), who was applying for grade two admission, had recently been diagnosed with Asperger's Syndrome.

Despite his high IQ scores, Peter was performing as an average student and intensive support was needed to ensure success in school. Previous school records reflected teacher anxiety and stress in getting Peter's cooperation. At the admissions committee meeting, all factors were discussed and the elementary school guidance counselor weighed in with his opinion.

"My heart goes out to Peter and his family, but it would be cruel for us to take him. He really should stay in Fairfax County, Virginia, where he is sure to get the kind of help he needs. His parents would be irresponsible to bring him here, to this school, in this country, where sufficient support is unavailable."

Around the table, Bill noticed many members of the admissions committee nodding their heads in agreement. He realized, at that particular time in the school's development, that Peter was not going to be able to succeed, because many of the adults who would have been responsible for his support and success really didn't want him there! As a school, ISKL had not yet developed the *will to serve*. Reluctantly, Bill conveyed the decision to the parents that ISKL was unable to serve Peter and he was denied admission.

Four years later, the same family re-applied for the admission of their two children to ISKL. It was a very different admissions committee that met this time. Each member of the admissions committee had come prepared and well-versed in Peter's case, and around the table individuals were asking questions like, "How can we make sure that Peter will succeed at ISKL?" "What supports do we need to put into place to serve him best?" "How can we make sure during breaks and lunch times that someone will check in with Peter to make sure he's OK?" "How might we prepare the teachers to make sure they know what to expect, and how they might approach him best?"

Clearly, the group was working towards establishing collaborative norms to support Peter, and it was evident that they were working towards admitting Peter and putting into place a plan to support his success in school.

Peter was admitted into grade six at ISKL. As often happens in cases like this, Peter's mother ran for the board of directors and was elected. Soon after her election, she made an appointment to see Bill. The purpose of her meeting was personal. Peter's mother said, "Bill, four years ago, you were the head of this school that denied admission to my son Peter. Four years later, we applied again, and this time, as head of this same school, you admitted him. Peter hasn't changed. Why wasn't he admitted the first time?"

Bill responded by saying, "Peter may not have changed, but in the last four years, the school has undergone a great change, and we have moved a long way towards becoming a more inclusive and more welcoming school. We're a different school from the one you applied to four years ago."

Schools can change. Teachers and school leaders can make the decision to become smarter in their work with all students, including those with special learning needs. Teaching faculties can develop expertise. We can all develop a will to serve. This represents the crucial intersection of technical and adaptive challenges, where informational learning supports and complements transformational learning.

What happened at ISKL in the intervening years was the experience of uncovering our capacity to succeed with special learners. Some of this was thrust upon the school by the court system in Malaysia, and others by our own realization that we were developing expertise and self-confidence in this area simultaneously as we developed a will and a passion to serve. We will shortly meet Amit and Ben, who were instrumental in helping ISKL develop a collective growth mindset. Their stories illustrate how students can serve to inspire and support the growth of organizational intelligence.

When we examine why a school might choose to deny admission to a child with special learning needs, several reasons emerge:

A fear of the unknown – how the admission of a child with learning needs will impact the culture of the school.

A fear of failure – the teachers', the school's and the students'.

Anxiety in respect to overly demanding parents.

Concern about how teachers will feel.

A lack of expertise or knowledge in working with diverse learners.

A lack of clarity surrounding the roles and responsibilities of the faculty, the administration, the parents, the student, and the community in working with children who learn differently – who is responsible for what?

A mis-conception that accepting students with special needs will somehow 'take away' from the learning of other students.

Confusion about the school's existing capacity to serve.

A need for certainty.

A desire to uphold the school's 'academic' reputation.

Complacency, or contentment with the *status quo.*

Fear of setting a precedent that may have far reaching educational and financial implications.

Many of these reasons overlap, often working in conjunction with one another. In chapter two we discussed the nature of fixed and growth mindsets (Dweck, 2008), and the attributes of schools exhibiting such mindsets. Many of the reasons given for the exclusion of students are characteristic of schools with fixed mindsets – schools that attribute their constraints and limitations to forces that they perceive to be outside of their control (limited professional expertise or resources).

For example, one of the easiest ways to uphold a school's reputation as an academically rigorous institution with good examination results is simply to restrict the type of student admitted. When enrolment is selective, the admissions policy is essentially a question of gate keeping - preserving examination results and entrance to prestigious universities that enhance the school's reputation. Our identity as a school is predicated on being learned, not on learning. Schools with collective fixed mindsets place a greater emphasis on *selecting* talent than on *developing* it.

There are times when schools may be disingenuous about their 'open' admissions. In one fairly large school we visited, the IB Diploma Programme coordinator very proudly told us that all students from the school, whoever wanted to, was admitted into the IB Diploma programme, and that for the last five years the school had maintained an average diploma point score of 38 (out of a possible maximum of 45).

We looked at one other with the same question: how is an average diploma point score of 38 possible to maintain with non-selective admissions? We later learned that students were being forceably exited at the middle school level. Several parents, some of them teachers, told us that their children had been exited before entry into the high school. Gate-keeping such as this can produce remarkable statistics, but does little to make schools collectively smarter. In fact, we see this as a form of cheating, a manipulation of numbers not too dissimilar to what transpired at Enron.

A fixed mindset causes an institution to become risk adverse. When a school exits students before high school or before the IB Diploma Programme, it suggests an unwillingness to take risks on children who might compromise the school's reputation and its high examination results.

A fixed mindset is evident when schools feel that they have to choose between being academically rigorous *or* being supportive of students with special educational needs. This is a false dichotomy. There is no need to choose between excellence and equity: we can have both (Tomlinson, 2003) and *be* both. As many flagship schools around the world are demonstrating, with the appropriate plans, structures and professional learning in place, we can provide an excellent and rigorous academic education for our students *and* be successful in our support of students with learning differences – a win-win situation.

In other situations, teachers and school leadership may be unaware of their own capacity for success, and may feel insecure about meeting the demands of working with students with special needs. Two students,

Amit and Ben, helped ISKL to discover its growing capacity to serve students with special learning needs.

What Amit and Ben taught the school

At an earlier point in the history of ISKL, the middle school faculty was faced with receiving two intensive needs students into grade six from the elementary school: a child who was wheelchair-bound with cerebral palsy, and another child with a developmental disability.

The middle school teachers baulked. They complained that they didn't have the professional preparation or the expert knowledge or skills required to work with Amit or Ben (not their real names). If teachers had to focus so much time and energy on just these two children, how would this affect the learning of other children?

It wasn't fair or right for the regular students. The administration took the teachers' side and invoked a rarely used line in the board policy manual: that 'admission into one section of the school does not guarantee admission into the next section'. Amit and Ben were asked to find other school placements for the following academic year.

In the ensuing chaos that resulted, one of the parents ran for the board and was ultimately appointed board chair; the second parent took the school to court and won an injunction (accompanied by much negative media scrutiny) against the school; two principals did not have their contracts renewed, and the head of school was fired.

To our knowledge, no head of school has ever been fired for being too inclusive. However, anecdotal evidence suggests the opposite to be true: heads of school are sometimes removed from their positions after a firestorm over the inclusion of special needs students. We have known several.

At ISKL, as teachers began working with Amit and Ben, and as their cases came up for review in student study team meetings, the middle school faculty slowly began to realize that both students, different as they were, were succeeding at school. 'Success' was measured in the social relationships the boys had with their peers, their success with academic work (some more limited than others), and their participation in extra-curricular activities. In short, were they happy at school? Were they learning? Were they growing as students?

Success was also measured by the increasing ease with which the faculty planned and handled their roles and responsibilities where these students were concerned. They were learning to differentiate instruction, and learning what could and couldn't be differentiated in terms of the curriculum; the difference between an accommodation and a modification, and how to go about making these decisions.

The teachers were engaged in the all important business of *un-masking* success, both theirs as well as the students'. Within 18 months, the faculty thought it was 'quite natural' for students like Amit and Ben to be at the school. Their capacity to work with diverse learners had increased, and the organizational intelligence of the middle school was enhanced. The faculty had moved from having a fixed to a growth mindset in regard to working with students with special needs.

Matthew and the middle school

We are reminded of another admissions case in which a family with four children applied to a school; the children were applying for spaces at the early years level, the elementary school, middle school and high school respectively. The admissions for the high school and early years children posed no problems and their admission was straightforward.

However, the children applying for elementary and middle school slots had intensive needs: both were late adoptees and had difficulties learning; previous report cards were full of the type of support that the children would need. The elementary school decision was to accept the child; given the structure of elementary classrooms, the principal thought they could manage the support the child needed.

But the middle school hesitated, and their first response was not to admit the child. The father, a senior employee from a major embassy, ran for the board of directors based on the admission of his other children – and was elected (as is often the case). He pressed the administration for the admission of his middle school child, and being wise to the political climate, the middle school made the prudent decision to accept Matthew (not his real name) into grade seven.

Teachers soon came to realize that Matthew had good social skills, and although he struggled academically, he 'fit' into the environment of the middle school. He had friends and he was working hard with a shadow teacher to meet the goals set in his individualized education plan (IEP). Teachers also worked to find expert knowledge and resources to support their instruction

At the end of term Matthew's parents attended a meeting with the student study team to discuss Matthew's progress and his settling into the school. Teachers were unanimous in their observation that Matthew had indeed made progress, and was considered 'one of the boys' in grade seven. All his teachers felt jointly responsible for his success in school. Furthermore, Matthew's learning was being supported not only by his teachers and the shadow teacher who had been privately hired, but also by his peer group. Matthew's progress was evident and measurable.

His parents were understandably pleased: "We knew this was the right place for Matthew, and you've shown us exactly that. Why didn't you admit him in the first place?" Members of the SST tried to explain that they had originally felt that Matthew would probably have had better access to the support and facilities available in the prestigious public school district that he had come from.

At that, Matthew's father exploded: "Please don't talk to me about sending kids to public school back home," he said. "I know what I'm talking about because we've just come from there. My children were in probably the best school district in the country and they were paid scant attention over the last two years.

"There was a lot of bureaucracy and a lot of paperwork to be done, a lot of hoops to jump through. It was almost March in their first year in the county before they received any help at all. International schools will do more for my children – just by the class size, the culture and the environment that you have here – than the schools they were in back home."

The experience of working with Matthew helped teachers at the school understand their capacity to work with children with special learning needs. Like the teachers at ISKL, they had developed a growth mindset.

It appears that children with special needs are here to stay and will remain a permanent feature of the international school landscape. Demographics have changed in the last few decades. Not long after the 1975 passage of Public Law 94-142 (otherwise known as the Education for All Handicapped Children Act) in the United States and other similar laws in the English speaking world, parents of children with special learning needs began to take up expatriate positions.

Not only did they bring their children with them, they also came with the expectation that their children would be welcomed at the school of their choice. Whereas previously, international schools really perceived a 'choice' in whether or not to serve these children, parental pressure has become a growing reality that has served as a catalyst for change.

So, whether we like it or not, special needs children are with us. We can be sensitive to our environment (de Geus, 1997) and look for opportunities to grow, given our changing demographics, or like the ostrich, keep our heads in the ground. Even schools with the tightest selective admissions policies barring the entrance of students with special educational needs will find that some will still make it past the admissions gate keeper. Perhaps they got through un-noticed or their learning difficulties may have surfaced later when the work became harder and more abstract. Even schools that explicitly deny children with special needs from enrolling may find surprises in their student populations.

So, how does a school become more open-minded? How does it develop a growth mindset and collective intelligence? Including students with special educational needs is one practical and explicit way of doing just that.

The AISJ story

The American International School of Johannesburg (AISJ) was recently faced with the opportunity to develop a growth mindset for serving children with special needs when a pre-school child with diagnosed disabilities on the autism spectrum applied for admission. The school's initial response was to reject Heather (not her real name), and the reasons given to the parents were that Heather had never been in an inclusive setting; that the school's recent attempts at inclusion had been challenging and not entirely successful; and that the school did not have the necessary supports in place.

After searching available resources in the Johannesburg area, Heather's parents found another placement for her, in a school that catered specifically for children on the autism spectrum. There were many benefits to this placement: there was a good therapist and Heather developed a positive relationship with her. Teachers were knowledgeable about autism and willing to learn about Heather's idiosyncrasies.

After some time, however, it became apparent that the academic program was not sufficiently challenging for Heather, and her social development stalled. Both parents and school recognized that Heather needed something more. With the school's support Heather's parents began the search for a new placement.

But this was a tough period for Heather and her family. Her parents discovered there were long waiting lists for private schools and that state schools in the area were under-resourced and over-crowded. They did find some remedial schools but even these were unwilling to take on the challenge of autistic learners.

And then, almost by fate, Heather's parents re-applied for admission to AISJ, and this time their reception was different. They were met by the new admissions coordinator and elementary school counselor, who took them on a tour of the campus and decided to advocate for Heather. A team of teachers visited Heather at her school and a managed and planned program of integration was developed.

Heather and her parents made several visits to AISJ and to the class where she was to be assigned, to meet the teacher and her future classmates. The class teacher had volunteered to have Heather in her class and spent the summer reading and studying about autism. The school and parents agreed that this was to be a trial period and that Heather would attend AISJ in the mornings, for half a day, and continue her therapy in the afternoons at her other school.

Taking the risk of serving Heather and others like her and meeting their needs is one of the factors that has helped the school to re-examine its mission in light of service to children with special needs. AISJ is in the process of re-defining its identity and reviewing its values as a school. Their vision is to challenge themselves to provide a quality education for all students, including students who represent greater learning diversity. The school is endeavoring to be more inclusive and sees this as a learning process.

* * * * *

What we hope is becoming evident in this chapter is that often schools hesitate to become more inclusive because making the decision to embark on that journey is akin to traveling as explorers of a different era into uncharted territory. There is no 'one right and only way' towards changing a school culture to be more welcoming to diverse learners. Like traveling to the moon, there are many unknowns and perhaps even unanticipated hazards along the way. But the goal is worthwhile and in the process, the challenges will provide opportunities for growth and enhanced collective intelligence. The journey begins with a decision, with open-mindedness, and in developing a will to serve.

The Next Frontier: Inclusion

Schools do not have to make this journey on their own. There are a number of international schools around the world that are already embarked on this journey, and many that are already sharing their learning at professional conversations hosted by The Next Frontier: Inclusion, an organization whose purpose is to support schools in becoming more inclusive. NFI is made up of a collaborative network of schools sharing a common belief that inclusion is the direction in which international education should grow. The goal is to realize one inclusive school in every major city around the world.

Inclusive schools (NFI, 2013) are defined as:

> Schools that successfully serve a managed number of students representing the full range of learning differences: mild, moderate, and intensive needs, and the exceptionally able.

Some of the key terms in this definition are 'successfully serve', 'a managed number' and 'representing the full range'. In other words, NFI does *not* advocate that schools accept all student applicants regardless of program availability, resources or student demographics. Inclusion does not mean that a child with Down Syndrome be placed in the same class as a student taking higher level math at the IB Diploma level.

NFI *does* advocate that schools carefully manage admissions to reflect the school's will to serve and its growing faculty expertise. No class or grade level should be overwhelmed with large numbers of students with special needs. Instead, NFI (Pelletier, Bartlett, Powell & Kusuma-Powell, 2011) suggests that at each grade level, school populations reflect the general population at large: 10-12% of students with mild learning disabilities, 2- 3% with moderate learning disabilities, and 1% with intensive special learning needs. Generally speaking, the 1% with special learning needs will require a separate program.

Resources and other publications supportive of inclusion in international schools are available on the Next Frontier: Inclusion website: www. nextfrontierinclusion.org/ Schools that subscribe to NFI share the following belief statements:

> High quality education is a basic human right of all children.

> We need to redefine international education to be inclusive of students who learn differently or at different rates.

> Parents who travel overseas should not have to leave some of their children behind or divide their families between schools.

> We are committed to a planned and carefully managed approach to including students who have special needs or may be exceptionally capable.

> The inclusion of children requiring learning support enhances the education of all children.

It is understood that schools will be at different developmental levels, at different stages in their respective journeys, in terms of their capacity to serve students with special needs. The important decision is to undertake the journey.

When we embrace the 'hard' goals – those that initially seem confusing, frightening, unrealistic or overwhelming, we engage individually and collectively in the process of redefining our professional identities. And when our values are clear, the decisions often take care of themselves.

Guided study questions

What might represent a 'hard' goal for your school? Under what conditions, could the pursuit of this goal enhance organizational intelligence?

The authors contend that the thoughtful inclusion of children with special learning needs requires a re-examination of our identity as an educational organization. In what ways is your schools currently engaged in re-examining its identity?

How do school leaders go about developing both the *capacity* and the *will* to serve students with special educational needs?

What opportunities does your school have for 'unmasking success'?

What does a collective growth mindset look and sound like? How do we go about developing collective Growth Mindsets in our schools?

Chapter 7

Leading adult learning

The central idea of this chapter is that there is a strong correlation between active learning and intelligence in both individuals and organizations. An individual who is actively engaged in learning something new and challenging is growing more intelligent than someone who is not so engaged.

The same is true, we would argue, for organizations. The concept of 'learning organizations' is not a new one (Senge *et al*, 2012) and a number of schools have embarked on collective learning initiatives. These include workshops, book study groups, interactive blogs and micro-teaching sessions. However most of these initiatives focus on informational, as opposed, to transformational learning.

In order for individuals to engage in transformational learning there needs to be a match between the developmental level of the individual and the supports and challenges that are provided (Drago-Severson, 2009). We will argue that the same is true for organizations such as schools – that in order for a school to engage in transformational learning (learning that affects the values, beliefs and identity of the school) leadership must identify the organization's developmental level and then design appropriate supports and challenges – what the McKinsey Report refers to as Stage Dependent Interventions (Barder et. al 2010).

Harvard psychologist Robert Kegan (1994) has developed a theory of adult development that has profound implications for school leadership and adult learning. Unlike some earlier psychologists, Kegan does not see mental and emotional growth ending in late adolescence. He sees human development as a lifelong, dynamic process of interaction of the individual and the environment.

Kegan's Constructive-Developmental Theory is based on how adults make meaning of the world around them. His basic idea is that as we grow cognitively and emotionally, the ways that we construct meaning become more and more complex. He bases his theory on three primary ideas:

Constructivism: Humans actively construct and make meaning of our experiences and create our realities with respect to cognitive, emotional, intrapersonal (the self's relationship to itself), and interpersonal pathways of development.

Developmentalism: The ways in which we make meaning and construct reality can develop over time and throughout our lifetime, provided that we benefit from developmentally appropriate supports and challenges.

Subject-object balance: This balance centers on the relationship between what we can take a perspective on – hold as an 'object' – and what we are embedded in and cannot see or be responsible for (are 'subject to'). Kegan argues that at different developmental stages, the subject-object balance changes as our ways of knowing become more complex.

For example, at a fairly concrete level of development, we might equate criticism with an attack on self and respond defensively. At this stage, it is not possible to get a perspective on the criticism. We are subject to it. As we grow, however, we see the world in greater complexity and we are able to take the same criticism and view it from multiple perspectives – perhaps as a helpful piece of advice from someone who cares for us. The criticism is no longer the subject, but has become the object. We are able to gain perspective on it.

Before we continue to explore Kegan's ideas about adult development and apply them specifically to schools, let's eavesdrop on a collective learning experience at the International School of the Pyrenees. As you read the case study, try to suspend judgment of the participants and ask yourself how their developmental level might be contributing to their behavior.

Essential questions and enduring understandings

Donald Noland finished his brief lecture on the basic principles of Understanding by Design. He was an experienced staff developer who had a well-deserved professional reputation in California. He had never worked outside the US before, but he sensed that the group of teachers from International School of the Pyrenees had a diversity of readiness levels.

Prior to the presentation, the headmaster explained that some of teachers were voluntarily present for the Saturday workshop, but others had been specifically 'sent'. The headmaster had joked that some of the teachers were in need of 'retreading'. Noland might expect some resistance.

"Now," Donald Noland smiled at the room full of faculty, "what questions are there?"

Marlene de Souza raised her hand. "I understand the three steps of backward design. I just don't know where to begin."

"You need to identify the desired learning results," Donald replied.

"But the curriculum should tell us that, shouldn't it?" Marlene's question reflected her confusion. She wanted to do the right thing. She felt a little frustrated that the expert seemed unwilling to share his expertise.

"For example," Noland asked, "what will you be teaching next week?"

Marlene hesitated only a moment: "We start our unit on the industrial revolution."

"Why should students learn about the industrial revolution?"

"Because it's important," Marlene wondered why Noland would ask such an obvious question. She felt a little uncomfortable, almost defensive. Why was the workshop leader singling her out for all this attention?

"And why is the industrial revolution important?" Noland attempted to probe deeper.

"Because it's in the curriculum."

Donald Noland took a deep breath. He understood that teaching at a conceptual level was a challenge to some teachers.

"We need to identify big ideas and concepts that will be truly valuable for students to know 20 years from now."

"Like what?" Nicole Rouge asked from the back of the room. "I teach French. There are no concepts in teaching French. You memorize the words and you learn the language. It's as simple as that, *n'est ce pas?*"

"But we all need to agree on the big ideas, don't we?" Allie Loupis asked. "I mean curriculum development needs to be a collaborative endeavor. We all need to be on the same page. We can't all go our individual ways?"

"Absolutely not," Noland went on. "Teachers need to come together and move from teaching topics to teaching concepts. Understanding by Design is based on conceptual teaching. A topic might be green plants, butterflies or frogs. A teachable concept, on the other hand, might be life cycles..."

"Who on earth teaches frogs?" Dimple Desai demanded. "That's disgusting."

"I teach frogs," Thomas Winchester announced. "We dissect frogs regularly in the bio lab."

"I suspect," the workshop leader went on diplomatically, "that Mr. Winchester uses frogs in the biology lab as the content to teach important concepts. You don't actually teach frogs."

"What are some of the similarities in the development of living things?" Old Benjamin mumbled beneath his breath.

"Exactly!" Donald Noland was delighted that at least one participant had grasped the idea of Understanding by Design. "You have framed an Essential Question."

"But how many other schools are doing this UbD thing?" Carey Legget asked.

"With all due respect, Dr Noland," Harold Robertson began, " I teach in the International Baccalaureate programme. I teach English language A1 at higher level. I have a syllabus to cover and I simply do not have the time to do all this unit planning and backward design stuff. I was hired to teach..."

"But we need to know what the big concepts are and the students need to know what the learning targets are," Allie Loupis added. "If the teacher isn't clear about what she is teaching the students will certainly be confused. Teaching at a conceptual level invites students to make intellectual connections..."

"May I ask why can't the administration of this school leave us alone so that we can get on with what we are trained to do?" Victoria Plum asked.

Lars Olsson looked at his shoes and Amy Fellows flushed with embarrassment.

"Victoria," Allie Loupis announced, "you make me ashamed of being part of this faculty."

While the school is hypothetical, all of the comments recorded in the above case study are taken from real life. If we suspend judgment on the discourteous behavior, we can explore what might be lurking beneath the surface of the conversation. While a few of the teachers (Allie Loupis and Old Benjamin) seem to understand and even embrace the ideas of Understanding by Design (Wiggins & McTighe 2000), others seem confused (Marlene D'Souza and Nicole Rouge) and some even appeared threatened by the idea and hostile to the consultant (Harold Robertson and Victoria Plum).

These different responses may have to do with the different developmental levels of the individuals concerned – quite literally how they make meaning out of the world around them.

Kegan's research suggests that the ways in which we construct meaning are not associated with gender, age, or life phase. Meaning making, what David Rooke and William Torbet (2005) refer to as 'action logic' is developmental and Kegan suggests to us that there are four developmental stages of adult life: instrumental, socializing, self-authoring and self-transforming.

Each of these developmental stages incorporates the former into its new, more expansive meaning-making system. Although this theory is hierarchical, one way of knowing is not necessarily better than another and Kegan stresses that an appropriate developmental stage matches the level of complexity of the environment, which is in essence a 'goodness of fit' model. He does, however, go on to point out that many of the complex demands of modern life outpace our developmental levels and many of us may be 'in over our heads' as we saw in the previous case study.

We would suggest that one of the most significant challenges facing schools around the world is that the really important educational outcomes (the dispositions and skills needed to thrive in our increasingly complex modern world) are beyond the developmental level of many schools.

Let's take a look at Kegan's four stages of adult development in greater depth.

The instrumental way of knowing: the 'rule-bound self'

The person at the instrumental stage of knowing has a very concrete orientation to the world. A person at this stage of development is defined by his or her own concrete needs, desires, and purposes. In general, an instrumental knower cannot take on the perspective of another person fully. Empathy is very limited.

Other people are perceived as either helpers or hinderers to getting one's own concrete needs met, and another person's needs are important only if they interfere with the desires of the instrumental knower. For example, an instrumental knower might be thinking: I have been teaching for eight years and haven't received a serious complaint. Now this new principal comes in with all his modern ideas! Perhaps if I show him that I like him he'll get off my back. The 'modern ideas' are perceived as a threat to the *status quo* and relationships are manipulated in order to meet self-oriented needs.

Teachers and school leaders at an instrumental level tend to be opportunistic; they look to win in any way possible. They can perceive other people as opportunities to be exploited and often have a strong need to control or direct the outcome of activities. They may reject feedback, externalize blame and respond with hostility to new or challenging ideas. There are several hints in the previous case study that the defensiveness of Victoria Plum and Harold Robertson may suggest an instrumental level of development.

People at the instrumental stage of knowing engage in dualistic thinking: they believe in right and wrong answers – 'right' ways to think and 'right' ways to act. They generally want to learn 'the rules' – whether the rules dictate how to teach a lesson, collaborate with colleagues, or design unit plans. Instrumental knowers have no understanding of shades of gray, irony or paradoxes. They also have no comprehension or tolerance for ambiguity. Marlene D'Souza's concrete responses to the curriculum questions may suggest an instrumental level of development.

The socializing way of knowing: 'the other-centered self'

The socializing stage of development is by far the largest and includes most older adolescents and adults. While the socializing stage represents fairly traditional thinking, the individual has the capacity to think abstractly and can identify with and internalize the feelings of others.

The socializing individual is also able to respond to the needs of others.

However, the socializing individual is driven by the opinions and perceptions of others. His or her wants are defined by other people's expectations. The socializing individual may actually feel responsible for the feelings of other people. The socializing stage of development is ideal for a tribal village where loyalty and stability are of paramount importance.

For the socializing knower interpersonal conflict is experienced as a threat to self; thus the socializing knower avoids conflict because it is a risk to the relationship. They can't provide critical feedback or make unpopular but necessary decisions. Rooke and Torbert (2005) refer to individuals at this stage of 'action logic' as diplomats who obey group norms (without real examination) and tend not to rock the boat.

The strengths of the socializing individual is that he or she provides cohesion to groups, attends to the needs of others, but often is unable to distinguish between positive teams and negative dysfunctional ones. Loyalty is a paramount virtue to the socializing teacher, often at the expense of critical thinking. Ineffective teams that may be characterized by cynicism and a lack of efficacy may be made up of socializing individuals.

The socializing teacher finds motivation and comfort in the approval and acceptance of others. These others might be students, colleagues, and supervisors. The socializing teacher will particularly seek to please and win the approval of higher status colleagues. The teacher who is at the socializing stage of development finds it fairly easy to take on the perceptions of colleagues and see the world through their eyes. When the school culture is positive, this can result in enhanced collaboration and collegiality. However, when there is a negative culture, the socializing teacher can be readily sucked into it.

Socializing teachers are quite conventional and traditional in their approach to classroom instruction, and while they want and need external validation (praise from colleagues or the principal), they often do not want to be so much in the limelight that they stand out from other teachers. The socializing teacher may also be reluctant to accept positions of responsibility that require making potentially difficult or unpopular decisions. We see this commonly when team leaders or heads of department adamantly refuse to have anything to do with the professional supervision of colleagues.

When socializing individuals are appointed to senior positions of leadership, the situation can become even more problematic as they will tend to ignore conflict and find it virtually impossible to provide challenging feedback. They are usually very poor at initiating school improvement plans because such changes will inevitably involve much dreaded conflict.

Leaders can have a very significant influence on the developmental level of organizations. Rooke and Torbert's (2005) research suggest that approximately 12% of organizations have socializing or diplomat leaders. However, their research was undertaken in the corporate sector. We suspect that in schools the percentage of socializing leaders is significantly higher. This may correlate to the intense resistance to change that we see in some schools.

The self-authoring way of knowing: 'the reflective self'

Kegan (1994) suggests that fewer than 50% of adults transition into the self-authoring stage. Self-authoring individuals have developed their own deeply-held values and internal set of rules. Self-authoring individuals are not necessarily dependent on others for evaluation or esteem.

They are more field independent in the sense that they are self-guided, self-evaluative, and self-motivated. They can be highly efficacious and tend to gravitate in schools towards positions of leadership and responsibility. They are not shy about embracing new ideas and may spearhead new initiatives.

There are several ways in which self-authoring individuals can present themselves. The first is with an authoritative emphasis on expertise. 'Experts try to exercise control by perfecting their knowledge, both in their professional and personal lives. Exercising watertight thinking is extremely important to experts...' (Rooke & Torbert, 2005, p6) They pursue continuous improvement and efficiency; on occasion they may lack flexibility and can be perceived as perfectionists. They may not have well developed interpersonal skills and emotional intelligence may not be highly valued. In addition, some may perceive collaboration as a waste of time.

Each summer Bill teaches at the Principals' Training Center and invites participants to reflect on their developmental journey as leaders. On one occasion a veteran principal related an anecdote about himself as a young administrator that may illustrate the emotional myopia of the 'expert stage'.

He was principal of a school in a remote location in Africa where it was impossible to get substitute teachers to cover for the illnesses and absences of colleagues. Accordingly, the young principal devised a 'substitute schedule' in which teachers would cover for absent colleagues. Soon after the schedule was posted in the staffroom, a small delegation of teachers came to the principal to complain that the schedule didn't distribute the burden of cover equitably.

The young principal's response: "You get a salary and you want fairness too!" The veteran school leader told the story on himself as an example of how everyone has the potential for developing greater emotional intelligence.

Research confirms that individuals can learn to combine professional expertise with high degree of emotional intelligence (Powell & Kusuma-Powell, 2010). When this occurs we see the emergence of what Rooke and Torbert (2005) call the Self-Authoring Achiever. These individuals can manage their feelings and emotions and are able to discuss their internal states. They are other-centered and sensitive to the social interactions of groups. They have the capacity to hold opposing feelings simultaneously. Self-authoring achievers have the capacity for reflection on their multiple roles as teachers, leaders, parents, partners and citizens. Competence, achievement, and responsibility are the uppermost concerns of people who make meaning in this way.

As teachers or school leaders, self-authoring achievers have internalized a series of values and beliefs about teaching and learning, and their professional behavior is guided by those values and beliefs. They are open to feedback and realize that many of the conflicts of everyday life may be the result of differences in perception and interpretation.

However, the self-authoring teacher may also be quirky and individualistic. They may tend to ignore rules and regulations that they regard as irrelevant, which may bring them into conflict with school leaders or colleagues. Prescribed curriculum may be bemoaned as inhibiting creativity and what are perceived as 'educational fads' may be greeted with skepticism. The self-authoring achiever is self-directed and self-evaluating and may actually find external direction and evaluation (including praise) de-motivating.

169

One of the hallmarks of a self-authoring achiever is the manner in which he or she deals with conflict. This is something that we will examine in greater depth when we look specifically at the developmental levels of schools.

The self-transforming way of knowing: 'the interconnecting self'

Kegan (1994) suggests that very few adults achieve the self-transforming stage of development, and if they do it is after the age of 40. Having said that, developmental stages are not linked to chronological age. This can create confusion and conflict in age-graded cultures where a younger person is at a more complex level of development than an older colleague or supervisor.

Kegan (1994) sees the self-transforming stage as ideal for a world that embraces complexity, chaos and interactive and adaptive systems. In some regards, the self-transforming stage shares similarities with Maslow's (1954) stage of self-actualization and Erikson's (1973) ego-integration. Self-transforming individuals are able to see beyond the limits of their own internal systems. They understand that perceptions are selected and constructed, have powerful influences over our behavior and decision-making, and are open to multiple and even contradictory interpretations.

These are individuals who are constantly inviting us to see things in a different way; to look for the assumptions that lie beneath our beliefs; and to examine the implications of those assumptions. Self-transforming individuals are able to tolerate and appreciate ambiguity and uncertainty. They tend to see grey instead of black and white. They are open to reconsidering and reconstructing what at first seemed clear and straightforward. They move from the known to the unknown, from certainty to uncertainty and their lives are rich in small and large ironies.

Self-transforming teachers are rare and they are often misunderstood by colleagues at less complex stages of development. They may be perceived as difficult and negative, out of touch with the mainstream, questioning for the sake of questioning, or simply not playing with a full deck. Kegan (1994) reminds us that being more complex than the society we live in can be dangerous. He is quoted as saying: "We loved Socrates, Jesus and Gandhi *after* we murdered them."

The self-transforming teacher has highly-developed internal values and beliefs and is able to integrate these with a sense of purpose that is larger than self. Autonomy and integration are seen as complementary processes. In other words, individualism is not perceived as the opposite to collectivism; being true to one's self is not necessarily opposed to being a subordinate member of a community or group; leadership and followership form a seamless dance. Self-transforming individuals avoid dichotomous thinking and understand that our sense of reality is based on perceptions and assumptions, and they examine, scrutinize and reflect on these assumptions.

In some respects the self-transforming individual has managed to develop what John Keats (in Fullan, 2001) referred to as 'negative capability'. The phrase has been wildly misunderstood, perhaps due to the use of the word 'negative'. The story goes that Keats was hosted to a dinner by an individual who was seemingly unable to address any subject without developing a strident and extreme opinion upon it.

Bored and irritated by his opinionated host, Keats reflected upon what it might be that compelled people into the fervent folly of such quests for certainty. He felt that the poet needed to develop negative capability, which was when an individual is capable of 'being in uncertainties, mysteries and doubts, without irritable reaching after facts and reasons" (Keats, 1899).

The Brazilian philosopher Roberto Unger (2004) perceives negative capability as liberating in that it empowers us 'against social and institutional constraints and loosens the bonds that entrap us in certain social stations'. The British psychoanalyst Wilfred Bion perceived the achievement of negative capability as being a way to temper existential angst. It is the ability to tolerate the pain and confusion of not knowing, rather than imposing ready-made or omnipotent certainties on ambiguous situations or emotional challenges (Symington & Symington, 1996).

The self-transforming teacher is less constrained by organizational taboos and will often consider such 'forbidden' topics or issues as discussable and transformable. Perhaps the most distinctive feature of self-transforming individuals is that they are motivated by the pursuit of wisdom and understanding.

Self-transforming school leaders, whether of a small team or a large organization, often project a 'developmental stance' (Rooke & Torbert, 2005). This means that they understand that adult development doesn't stop at the end of adolescence but continues over the lifetime. They have witnessed such growth in themselves and now seek out opportunities to support such growth in others.

Self-transforming school leaders are often intuitively aware of the developmental stages of colleagues and provide them with appropriate 'holding environments'. In other words they provide appropriate supports (psychological safety) and challenges for the specific stage of development. This serves to enhance collaboration, prevent destructive personalized conflict and minimize resistance to innovation; and often makes self-transforming individuals very effective change agents.

Summary of Kegan's stages of adult development*

Instrumental	Socializing	Self-Authoring	Self-Transforming
Many adolescents and some adults	Some older adolescents and most adults	Fewer than half of adults	Very few adults, usually after the age of 40.
Are motivated by concrete needs, interests and wishes	Can internalize the feelings of others and are guided by them.	Have developed an internal set of rules.	See beyond the limits of their own systems.
Oriented to self-interests.	Able to abstract and respond to needs other than their own	Internal governing system for decision-making and conflict resolution.	Perceive grey as opposed to black and white
Are rule based. Looking for the 'right' answer, the "right" way to do things.	The expectations of others define what I want	Not dependant on others for evaluation or esteem	Devoted to something beyond themselves
Decisions are based on self-interest.	Decisions are based on what others think.	Decisions are based on internal values and beliefs.	Decisions take into account complexity. Individual is able to look across systems.
Guiding questions: What's in it for me? Will I get punished?	Ideal for tribal village model where loyalty to the group is paramount.	Ideal for a diverse and mobile world focused on science and the search for truth.	Ideal for a world that rejects objectivity and embraces subjectivity, complexity, chaos and interactive systems.

*Adapted from *Leading Adult Learning* (2010) by E. Drago-Severson, Corwin Press and *Becoming an Emotionally Intelligent Teacher* (2010) by W Powell & O Kusuma-Powell, Corwin Press.

A metaphor for a developmental model

When we teach the stages of adult development, students are inclined to think of them as a hierarchical ladder, with increased value ascribed to the more complex levels. This provides a far too linear and sequential model for a process that is actually recursive and iterative. To some extent developmental levels are situational and there is a strong suggestion that at times of strong emotional stress we may revert to simpler ways of making meaning. There is also the suggestion that the transition from one stage to another may involve a time of cognitive and emotional turbulence and trauma.

Kegan (1994) presents his model of adult development as a helix, a spiral that curls back and revisits itself.

Our friend and colleague Toni Prickett suggests that an even more appropriate model may the increasing complexity of a fractal. Take for example rock crystals, snowflakes, DNA or even Romanesco broccoli; the original design is recapitulated in increasing complexity in each iteration. The previous stage is incorporated into the new level. So, when applied to adult development, we don't actually move from stage to stage, the previous stage is incorporated into the new, more complex one.

In the next chapter, we will explore how groups and organizations may have specific developmental levels and how these stages may play out in the day to day life of our schools.

Guided study questions

What are some implications for school leaders of Kegan's stages of adult development?

To some extent, the stages of adult development are situational. In what situations are we likely to see growth? In what situations are we likely to see regression?

In what ways can a group encourage its members to engage in self-exploration?

Case study: 'Joy to the World'

A log fire burned merrily in the stone fireplace at the far end of the faculty lounge. It was, Amy Fellows reflected, the only thing merry in the school. In an effort to introduce some Christmas cheer, she had brought in the spruce boughs that lined the mantle and had hung the multi-colored paper chains that festooned the vaulted timber ceiling. In the background, Bing Crosby could be heard softly extolling the virtues of a white Christmas. While there was little chance of a white Christmas in Ethiopia, Amy fervently hoped the holiday season would bring joy, peace and good will to the much-divided faculty of the International School of the Pyrenees

Yesterday Amy had mustered all of her courage and had had a private conference with the headmaster. She had rehearsed carefully what she was determined to say. She was nervous and had no idea how Eddie would respond to her. After some preliminary pleasantries, Amy told Eddie Rosencrantz that she respected what he was trying to accomplish at the school. She shared many of his values and beliefs about learning.

However, she went on to say that his brusque manner had alienated some teachers. Her lower lip trembled as she spoke. She thought he should spend more time in the faculty lounge. He should let people get to know him. She said she thought people misunderstood him because they hadn't had a chance to really get to know him. She concluded by inviting him to the faculty lounge to have a glass of her homemade eggnog.

At the end of the conference, Eddie had smiled at Amy and told her she was a very courageous young woman and that he would take her advice seriously. It really seemed that Eddie had taken her advice to heart.

The previous four months had been difficult ones at the school. Rex Butcher was in the midst of summarizing his perceptions of the situation. A dozen or so teachers sat before the fire in the faculty lounge listening.

"In my mind, you're either part of the problem or part of the solution. Know what I mean. Rosencrantz is systematically destroying this school and the people in it. Just look at staff morale. It's at an all time low. We've got to do something. In numbers there's strength. The board will listen if the teachers speak with one voice. And that voice isn't our fearless staff association president. She's in bed with the enemy."

Several teachers chuckled bitterly. Amy bit her lip. She hated the rumors and gossip.

"He's trying to run us off and it's not going to work. I need this job," Rex added vehemently.

"You're absolutely right, Rex." Victoria Plum spoke with considerable passion. "He's undermining everything that this school has stood for. He observed my class yesterday and afterwards he sent me an email with what he called 'suggestions for improvement'. Why can't the man leave us alone to get on with what we were trained to do?"

"He did the same in my French class last week," Nicole Rouge announced. "Has he observed your class, Lars?"

Lars Olsson looked up from the newspaper he was reading. He tried to avoid being drawn into these discussions.

"Eddie observed two of my lessons last month," Lars responded. "We had a conversation about them afterwards."

"And?" Nicole demanded.

Lars shrugged. "Afterwards Eddie asked me some questions."

"What questions?" Victoria asked.

"He told me that during the lesson I had spoken to nine out of the 14 students directly and he asked me how I had made the decision which students to call upon."

"You see he's trying to find fault in everything," Victoria added.

"He's got a hit list," Rex interjected.

"He didn't sound critical, just interested," Lars responded. "Although he's sometimes abrasive, I think Eddie really cares about student learning. At the end of the conversation, I suggested to him that he take it a bit easy with the faculty. Rupert Kingsley-Greene was a popular head of school. Taking over from him hasn't been easy for Eddie. I suggested that he take things a bit slower."

Amy found herself nodding in agreement.

"What did he say?" Old Benjamin called from an overstuffed armchair in the corner of the fireplace. Old Benjamin was an enigma – an ancient, white-haired, metaphysical poet who taught Theory of Knowledge and spoke in riddles. Most of the time he infuriated people by asking if what they said was fact, truth, theory, opinion or assumption and how they knew the difference. He was the butt of many faculty jokes.

"Rosencrantz said he wasn't going to enter a popularity contest with Kingsley-Greene. He said he wasn't concerned about whether he was liked or not by the faculty. In fact, he actually said that he was gratified by some of the push back he had been receiving from a few staff members. He said that it indicated that his message was being heard."

"He's a perverse bugger," Rex interjected.

"He told me he cares greatly for student learning and that would be his touchstone." Lars turned back to his newspaper. The Israelis were building more settlements in east Jerusalem and the Palestinians were threatening another *infitada*. Child's play, he mused, next to the hardening positions at the International School of the Pyrenees.

"All Eddie cares about is Eddie," Rex snapped back.

"What other ways might there be to interpret Dr Rosencrantz's behavior? Could his motivation be more complicated than that?" Old Benjamin asked softly.

"Oh get a life Benjamin!" Rex dismissed the older man.

"Complicated my foot!" Victoria was in high dudgeon. "The man is an absolute menace!"

"And which man might that be?" Eddie Rosencrantz grinned from the doorway. "At Amy's invitation, I have dropped by for some eggnog. She thought that some Christmas cheer would do us all good. Joy to the world and all that."

"Where angels fear to tread," Old Benjamin murmured beneath his breath.

Discussion questions

What evidence do you see of Kegan's Stages of Adult Development among the various characters at the International School of the Pyrenees?

In what ways might the interaction between characters be influenced by differing stages of development?

Chapter 8

Schools have developmental stages, too

Like individuals, organizations develop. There are young and relatively simple organizations and there are mature and complex ones with every shade of difference represented in between. There also appears to be a bi-directional relationship between the developmental level of the school and the developmental level of the teachers and school leaders. We say bi-directional because while it is obvious that developmental levels of individuals will influence the group, it is also true that the maturity and complexity of the group has a profound influence on the individual.

Differentiated organizational learning

The developmental stages of schools and school systems has been most recently and most powerfully illustrated in the so-called McKinsey Follow Up Report (Barber *et al*, 2010). The report identifies 20 school systems worldwide that have achieved continuous improvement over time. Not all of these were great or excellent (in fact some were still in the fair or good category) but all had achieved steady improvement over time.

The authors of the report were interested in what these school systems were doing right and so they undertook an in-depth analysis looking for significant variables. They found that there were two types or categories of interventions that supported these schools' improvement. The first category they labeled Cross Stage Interventions.

These were interventions that were required irrespective of the school's stage of development. Every school needs to have them. Cross stage interventions included revising curriculum and standards; ensuring appropriate rewards and remuneration structures for teachers and principals; assessing students; establishing data systems and facilitating improvement through the introduction of new policies.

However, the authors of the McKinsey Follow Up Report also found a second category of intervention that was critical to continuous school improvement. This they labeled Stage Dependent Interventions. In other words, schools at different stages of development require different interventions in order to continue to improve. In short, like students and teachers, organizational learning needs to be differentiated.

The Report identified four stages of school development, which they labeled to correspond to the school's systems results on international standardized tests (PISA): Poor to Fair; Fair to Good; Good to Great; and Great to Excellent.

The most effective interventions for schools in the Poor to Fair category were focused on supporting students in achieving basic literacy and math skills. These interventions include direct instruction and scaffolding for teachers with low skill levels and a high degree of centralized control.

In the Fair to Good schools the most effective interventions had to do with consolidating systemic foundations including the gathering of high quality performance data, ensuring teacher accountability, creating appropriate financing, organization structures, and pedagogical models.

Note that in these two categories the intervention tends to be externally derived and focused on teacher behavior and capabilities (the most basic levels of Embedded Learning). When we move to the final two categories, the interventions tend to be derived more internally (for both individuals and collective groups) and focus on values, beliefs and identity. External accountability is transformed into an internal sense of responsibility.

In schools in the Good to Great category, the most effective interventions had to do with ensuring that teachers and school leadership were regarded as members of a full-fledged profession; that they were treated with dignity and respect. Schools were seen to be implementing career paths and necessary practices to ensure that the profession was as well defined as medicine or law.

Finally in the schools that were seen to be in the Great to Excellent category, the focus was peer-based learning and promoting system sponsored innovation and experimentation. These were the so-called 'lab schools' that were truly transformational and generative.

Taking a closer look at the stages of school development

One of the most frequent causes of destructive conflict in schools between faculty and leadership can center on misunderstandings about development levels.

For example, a well-established school with a majority of faculty at a self-authoring stage of development appoints a new principal. The principal is at a socializing stage of development and looks for his values and beliefs about teaching and learning from others. He has a very affiliative leadership style and seeks the approval of the staff. He avoids conflicts and finds it extremely difficult to give critical feedback. He also struggles when faced with making unpopular, but necessary decisions.

There is a two to three month honeymoon period and then the staffroom begins to buzz with criticism of the new principal. Teachers are wondering where his leadership is and whether he's involved in a popularity contest. It is not long before the faculty are openly questioning the competence of the new principal and organizational trust is eroded.

Let's take a look at the opposite situation: a relatively young school, with a predominantly socializing faculty, appoints a new principal who is at a self-authoring stage of development. The new principal arrives with a set of well-developed and strongly held values and beliefs about teaching and learning. He has a dynamic vision for the school and is impatient to take it forward. He wants to put his mark on the school and place the school on the map!

The few self-authoring teachers recognize that while his manner may be a bit brusque, his heart is in the right place and his vision is compelling. Not so, unfortunately, the majority of socializing teachers: all they are aware of is his perceived rudeness and appalling lack of appreciation for his teachers. He is perceived as cold, arrogant, self-centered and lacking respect for the faculty. Organizational trust is eroded.

Our estimate of developmental levels of international school principals and heads of school*

Level of development	Principals	Heads of school
Instrumental	1-2%	Less than 1%
Socializing	40-65%	20-40%
Self-authoring	20-40%	40-65%
Self-Transforming	Less than 1%	1-2%

*These figures are the product of an informal survey of international school administrators. However, given the self-selected nature of international school leaders (*ie* those who have chosen the adventure of leading a school in a country other than their own, the percentage of self-authoring individuals may be higher than those in national systems).

Holding environments and organizational growth

Individual and organizational growth emerges in an appropriate 'holding environment' (Drago-Seversen 2009), one that presents appropriate supports and challenges for the developmental stage. Individuals and groups need psychological safety in order to embrace the cognitive and emotional discomfort that is often associated with growth and change.

There are five knowledge domains to teaching and learning (Powell & Kusuma-Powell, 2011). Each can comprise a rich arena of professional inquiry. They include:

Knowing your students as learners.

Knowing your curriculum.

Knowing your pedagogical strategies.

Knowing your assessments.

Knowing your collegial interactions.

Each of these knowledge domains provides a rich and challenging topography for professional exploration and growth. However, to maximize the learning experience, individuals and groups require support.

In terms of such support, we know that in schools there four basic functions or roles that colleagues can employ for each other. These are coaching, consulting, collaborating and evaluating (Costa & Garmston, 2002). The intention of each is different and may or may not be effective depending upon the developmental level of the individual or group. In fact, the developmental stage of schools can be characterized by the predominance of one kind of support over another. Let's look closely at the four support functions:

The intention of coaching (we are referring specifically here to Cognitive Coaching^{sm}) is to support the thinking of a colleague. The coach does not offer advice, solutions, ideas or judgments. The belief is that the individual or group has all the resources needed to plan, reflect, or resolve problems. Coaching focuses on transformational, self-directed learning.

Consulting is when an expert is called in to give advice, offer ideas and generate solutions. The intention of consulting is to transmit useful knowledge and generally involves informational learning. Consulting can appeal to instrumental individuals and groups since the premise is that there is best (or at least 'better') practice and a right way to do something.

Collaboration is when two or more individuals come together as equals, irrespective of positions of authority, to engage in a common task. There is a collective sense of responsibility and individuals in the group share accountability for outcomes.

Collaboration may represent a desirable challenge for instrumental groups, but the norms and skills need to be taught explicitly and practiced self-consciously. Many of the norms of collaboration require individuals to engage in flexible thinking (to take on the perspectives of others); this can be a useful stretch for instrumental individuals and groups.

The purpose of evaluation is to ensure compliance. The assumption is that there are standards for the execution of professional behavior and compliance to these standards is best achieved through regular external evaluation and judgmental feedback. Instrumental individuals and groups may actually find such evaluation (even if it involves some criticism) comforting since it is frequently based on the idea that there is a right and wrong way to do things.

This may appeal to their fairly concrete thinking. The danger of external evaluation is that research (Sanford, 1995) has shown that it inhibits self-assessment and self-directedness. Instrumental individuals should be encouraged to self-evaluate, although they may initially find the expectation uncomfortable.

Obviously most schools are combinations of different developmental levels depending on the situations and challenges they may face. Nevertheless it is often useful to have a general model to guide our inquiry. Let's explore schools at different stages of development.

Instrumental schools: rule-bound organizations

Instrumental schools operate at the simplest common denominator. Their success indicators are quantifiable and usually fall into two categories: examination results (test scores) and financial viability. These are essentially mechanical organizations, collections of assets in which input is compared to output and the proverbial the bottom line is standardized test scores or in proprietary schools, shareholder profit.

One of the easiest and most telling barometers of a school's development level is simply to ask the stakeholders how they define school success. In instrumental schools the stakeholders have often not given this much explicit thought and may seem confused or put off by the question. When there is an answer forthcoming, it is often monolithic (*eg* entry to prestigious universities).

Instrumental schools fall into various categories. There are simply young schools that have not yet had the opportunity to develop and clarify values, beliefs, traditions and mission. There are also older schools than are kept artificially immature by large and frequent turnover of leadership, teachers or board members. Some international schools are frozen at an instrumental level because they operate in very remote hardship locations, staffed with young inexperienced teachers with very frequent turnover. There are also schools that are kept at an instrumental level by so-called strategic directives from the 'central office' and government ministries of education.

Instrumental schools are rule bound. They have large policy manuals, the lion's share of which deals with personnel and financial matters. Student disciplinary codes are extensive with prescribed consequences for infractions. Instrumental schools are wedded to doing things by the book.

These rules and regulations are often expressed as behavioral dos and don'ts (not as expectations that can reflect values). Instrumental schools engage in black and white thinking. We see evidence of instrumental thinking when we find 'zero tolerance' policies.

The media recently reported two examples of the folly of such absolute policies. The first was the case of the eighth grade boy who was suspended for ten days from a public school in Orlando, Florida, for presenting his French teacher with a bottle of wine as a Christmas present (Orlando Sentinel, Jan 17, 1998). The school had a zero tolerance policy for alcohol on campus.

More recently, a Florida lifeguard lost his job for leaving his assigned stretch of beach to rescue a drowning man 100 meters outside his area of responsibility (Jonsson, 2012). Instrumental organizations often focus on the algorithm, not on the larger meaning behind it; policy statements are sacrosanct and there is a prevailing fear of setting precedents. Very few sensible exceptions are made to the rules.

In schools at an instrumental stage of development, there is a belief that there is one way of doing things – the right way. Any other way is by definition wrong, deviant, counterproductive or inefficient. The 'right way' to do something, whether it is teaching reading or planning units of study, can take on a moral dimension. In other words, the 'right way' to do something is also the 'moral way' and to deviate from the right way is to hurt children.

We see this kind of thinking time and time again in the passionate debates that have focused on a Whole Language approach to reading as opposed to Phonemic Awareness or teaching mathematics conceptually as opposed to memorizing multiplication tables. We also see the instrumental approach when rigidity crowds out common sense: for example, when schools or curricular programs demand that primary teachers teach six units each year and that each unit must be six weeks long.

In instrumental schools teacher supervision is primarily evaluation-based on a prescribed checklist of observable teacher behaviors or standardized test scores or some combination thereof. The process claims to be objective and free from subjectivity; all teachers, irrespective of expertise or experience, are treated in the same fashion and therefore there is a superficial perception of fairness.

Feedback to teachers is reduced to comments about how the teachers exceed, meet or fail to meet the prescribed standards. Less formal feedback is also judgmental, usually consisting of statements of praise or criticism. Teacher motivation is also external; merit pay may be in place.

Instrumental schools tend to interpret the concept of human resources literally and view teachers merely as an expendable means to an end, rather than a human work community. We recently visited a proprietary school in which the director had just met with the full staff. He explained to the teachers that the owners (a large for-profit consortium) had decided that the curriculum of the school would change from British to American effective at the start of the next year. But, he went on to add, the good news was that that some of the teachers would probably be able to make the shift and everyone was welcome to re-apply for their jobs. (Footnote: teacher morale understandably plunged and the director was held responsible. He didn't make it to the end of the year. In instrumental schools everyone is expendable.)

If there is any professional learning in an instrumental school, it is informational and probably directly focused on the introduction of some new basal readers or math scheme. Instrumental schools often tend towards teacher-proof curricular programs and there may be low expectation for teacher cognition and creativity. There is also a tendency towards reductionism and immediate gratification. Therefore the school may be either fossilized and fairly immune to change or subject to frequent educational fads and the frustration of not seeing immediate improvement. Collegial support in instrumental schools is almost exclusively evaluation (even consulting becomes judgmental).

So-called strategic planning is reduced to fairly meaningless quantifiable results. Bill once facilitated a governance-training workshop at an international school in Africa. When the question of strategic planning was tabled, the head of school and the board proudly announced that they had one and only one strategic objective and it wasn't going to change: to raise the Iowa Test Scores by 2% each year.

While the collective commitment to student achievement may have been laudable, neither the head nor the board members could explain how this increase in ITBS scores represented meaningful learning on the part of a very internationally diverse group of students. (Footnote: the board members changed, the head's contract was not renewed and the school soon embarked in a much more meaningful conversation about mission and outcomes.)

Perhaps one of the most telling hallmarks of a school's development level is how it responds to conflict. We know that in human organizations, conflict is inevitable and when managed well can actually be very healthy and raise organizational intelligence. Because instrumental schools and those who lead them have great difficulty seeing situations from the perspective of other people, miscommunication and misunderstanding are frequent.

There may not be the collective ethos of presuming positive intentions on the part of other people. As a result, conflicts are often emotional and personalized. Even more significantly, when personalized conflict does emerge in instrumental schools, power is employed to resolve it. In instrumental schools we see conflict resolution, not conflict management. The outcome very often produces winners and losers: my way or the highway, causing bitterness and resentment and sowing the seeds for the next round of destructive conflicts.

Instrumental schools may have prevailing negative narratives, superficial adult-to-adult relationships, students who are almost exclusively motivated by extrinsic rewards, coercive classroom climates (grades are used extensively to reward and punish students), and toxic cultures that are filled with mistrust and suspicion. Trust is not highly valued and is readily compromised in the pursuit of expediency.

Socializing schools

Socializing schools represent genuine work communities. There may be a sense of common identity and group cohesion is a primary concern. However, the cohesion is conviviality – the pleasure of one another's company. The values and beliefs of the socializing school are external: the mission and expectations come from outside sources: accreditation agencies, curriculum organizations (such as the IB) and the practices of other schools. Values such as community service and an appreciation of cultural diversity and international mindedness are paid lip service, but there is little real enthusiasm or passion for them.

A primary, albeit unspoken, goal in socializing schools is not to rock the boat. Any change or innovation may be perceived as threatening the existing social structure. Group cohesion takes precedence over everything else, including student learning, critical thinking and craftsmanship. We see this when a master teacher finds it socially necessary to hide her light under a bushel, to mask expertise so that she does not stand out from her peers.

Socializing groups are often ineffective at planning, reflecting and problem resolving. They may tend to come to agreement too quickly because they are uncomfortable with unresolved issues and want quick answers and solutions. They may perceive a self-authoring member as being negative or even cynical when in fact the person may be the conscience of the group.

Socializing schools are very susceptible to groupthink (Janis, 1972) This phenomenon was first identified in the 1970s by the psychologist Irving Janis when he noticed the propensity of some groups to social cohesion at the expense of rigorous critical thinking. As a result, these groups tend to come to premature agreement and their decision-making may be seriously flawed.

Research has been undertaken to explore whether groupthink may have been responsible for misguided historical decisions (for instance not taking the Japanese threat to Pearl Harbor seriously; to launch the Challenger Space Shuttle; to approve the Bay of Pigs Invasion, and perhaps even the more recent American invasion of Iraq).

The symptoms of groupthink include:

The illusion of invulnerability ("We know what's best for the children. We're the professionals.")

Shared stereotyping ("The administration just doesn't care." "You know how the parents are in this community.")

Rationalization ("If it's not broken, don't fix it.")

The illusion of morality ("If they only knew what was really in children's best interest…")

Self-censorship ("I did have some questions and doubts, but everyone else seems to be OK with the idea.")

The illusion of unanimity (Well, we all seem to be in agreement.")

Direct pressure to conform ("Are you with us or against us?" "Why are you always so negative?")

Mind guarding ("I don't have the experience, knowledge, expertise to comment.")

There are some well-researched guidelines that groups can use to avoid groupthink. Expectations for group members might include:

When a group member has pertinent ideas or experience, express them.

Avoid premature advocacy.

Practice active listening and try to understand what others are saying. Paraphrase.

Practice pausing – it slows down the conversation and gives participants permission to think.

Realize that there is seldom one right plan, decision, answer, or approach. Know when to assert and when to integrate.

When you have feelings that are relevant, let the group know.

Make an effort to understand the big picture – the needs or vision of the whole school.

Manage –don't avoid – conflict within the group. Keep it in the cognitive domain. Establish norms for dealing with confrontation.

Distinguish between goals and strategies. Hold the goals constant, manipulate the strategies.

Appoint a so-called 'devil's advocate', someone specifically assigned to critique the ideas on the table. Periodic devil's advocacy role playing is excellent training for developing analytical skills, effective communication and emotional intelligence (Kreitner & Kinicki, 2010).

Professional development (PD) does take place in socializing schools, but it is not always very effective. In an effort to appear fair, professional development funding may be divided among faculty on an annual basis. Individual teachers are allocated a set amount of money, which they can then use to attend workshops or conferences. These conferences and workshops may or may not relate to the larger professional learning needs of the school. Because the use of PD funding is determined by the individual teachers, the organizational pattern of learning may be fragmented and lacking cohesion.

Socializing schools commonly join the PD bandwagon. Curriculum mapping, Understanding by Design, or differentiation can become the flavor of the month because other schools are focused on these areas. PD workshops are scheduled but connections between initiatives are not made explicit and therefore PD appears to be a smorgasbord of fragmented themes.

The lack of apparent coherence often results in teacher complaints about there being too much on their plates. There also may be little transfer from the workshop setting to implementation in the classroom.

The professional learning areas are often set externally, for example by accreditation agencies. There tends to be little intrinsic understanding of what PD initiatives are and how they might benefit student learning. In some socializing schools, professional learning is tolerated, but seen as an intrusion.

Socializing schools are very susceptible to external pressures and pressure groups. If other schools are doing it, it must be the right thing to do.

About ten years ago Bill went on an accreditation visit to a school in Melbourne, Australia, that had embarked on an ambitious one-to-one laptop program. However, this was before the school had installed wireless and each of the classrooms had to be reconfigured for the wiring with rows of desks bolted to the floor. This effectively cut out any cooperative or collaborative learning.

There had been no preparation of the teaching staff, and most had no idea how to incorporate laptops into their units of study. Bill's observation was that most students were using the laptops to play games unrelated to the classroom or watch movies. When he asked the head of school about the one-to-one initiative, the response was that other schools in Melbourne were doing it and his school had to be seen to be on the 'cutting edge'.

International school administrators commonly use electronic list serves such as Headnet and AISHnet to find out what other schools are doing. On one level, this makes great sense. If a sister school has developed a program or procedure that is working well and is willing to share it, why reinvent the wheel? However, another pattern may also be involved. Sometimes, the request takes on the nature of a survey that suggests that if something is common practice it must be good practice – even if it is unexamined practice.

A common fallacy in socializing schools is that, because we have talked about something, we have actually addressed it. On another accreditation visit to a school in Europe, Bill asked about the vertical articulation of the curriculum. The response: "Absolutely, that's been on the agenda of the senior management team several times just this last year." But nothing had been done about it. Socializing schools don't tend to address the 'so what' question?

Socializing schools may use platitudes in place of rigorous analysis and critical thinking. Teachers claim to promote student inquiry, but don't actually know how to inquire themselves. So-called units of inquiry are devoid of critical thinking. Teachers in socializing schools may be very uncomfortable teaching anything that they are still confused about.

Socializing schools tend to be risk-averse. In admissions decisions of children with special needs we will often hear the use of platitudes to justify risk avoidance. We hear statements such as "we can't be all things to all people" or "if this child is admitted, other students will suffer" or "the teachers will be overloaded". Any of these statements may be true, but the conclusion in socializing schools is reached before the rigorous examination and analysis is undertaken.

Socializing schools tend to have ineffective teacher supervision and the leadership tends to avoid the unpleasantness of counseling out ineffective teachers. This is often excused by invoking the host country labor laws. You can't fire teachers in Austria, Germany *etc*. Again the statement may be true, but in the socializing school it is used as an excuse to avoid confronting the marginal teacher. In order to preserve an illusion of fairness, teacher supervision in socializing schools may strive to be objective. Any hint of subjective criticism (praise is always welcomed in socializing schools) makes the individual involved in the process uncomfortable. We may hear teachers respond to feedback with statements like "Well, that's just your opinion" (the implication being that all opinions are equally valid).

As a result, those attributes of teaching and learning that are included in the teachers' evaluation are those that are most easily observable and quantifiable (attendance records, time on task, standardized test scores, *etc*).

For socializing schools conflict is often monolithic. It is perceived as destructive because it can damage relationships. For the most part, socializing schools avoid conflict – both affective and cognitive conflict. Socializing work teams may have great difficulty distinguishing between assertion and aggression. They may ignore conflict by pushing it under the table or when it is impossible to ignore, ascribe it to some immutable bad chemistry.

However, socializing schools can be respectful workplaces with a positive climate and pleasant relationships. But student learning is rarely the top priority. In socializing schools the priority is teacher employment and this can develop into 'us/them' adversarial relationships between teachers and administration.

A pseudo-trust can come to exist in a socializing school – it is based on collegial loyalty as opposed to a shared vision and mission. We hear this collegial loyalty when teachers say that criticism of a colleague is unprofessional even when student learning is being seriously compromised.

What supports and challenges are appropriate for socializing schools? One of the most profound needs of socializing individuals and groups is the positive approval of colleagues and supervisors. Socializing teams need encouragement and emotional support. One way to accomplish this is through paraphrasing.

Elizabeth Cohen (1997) studied the influence of social status on student learning in the classroom. She found that students with lower social status (less physically attractive, less popular, less academically successful) learned less. Her research suggests that teachers can influence student social status in the classroom. Teachers can actually mediate student status by identifying something a low status student has done well or something insightful he or she has said and draw public attention to it.

An extremely effective way of doing this is by using the paraphrase. When teachers paraphrase students in front of the class, they send the message that the student's contribution to the conversation is valuable and worthy of attention.

This is also applicable to adult work groups. A skillful facilitator will paraphrase individual contributions to a conversation and craft from them a unified group summary. This process supports socializing groups.

In addition socializing teams need to be conscious to presume positive intentions in order to ensure psychological safety. Gentle, but directive behavior can be effective. Socializing groups often need facilitation that provides structure, organization, values, beliefs and vision.

In order to grow, socializing schools also need challenges. These can take the shape of mediative questions that reflect the five states of mind, particularly questions that focus on flexibility and consciousness. Challenges may also include learning how to be assertive, distinguishing between cognitive and affective conflict. For example, ask a socializing individual to take on the role of devil's advocate. School leaders might model critical thinking and public adult learning. Socializing groups will also benefit greatly from explicit practice in the norms of collaboration.

Self-authoring schools

Self-authoring schools are purposeful work communities with clearly defined mission and values. There is a sense in self-authoring schools that the school culture is not something that happens to us, but rather something that we can take control over. The teachers are not subject to the school's narrative, they are its collective authors. There is a sense of collective efficacy: if we don't like the story as it is being told, we can change it.

In self-authoring schools we see a shift from a focus on teaching behavior to a focus on learning – for both students and teachers. There is also a move away from teaching as private practice (closed doors and unit plans as private intellectual property) to teaching as collaborative practice. There is often common planning time provided in the master schedule, and common assessment activities are the norm.

Increasingly in self-authoring schools improvement is not looked upon as an option but as a requirement, and accountability (external evaluation and monitoring of standards) is replaced by internally-held responsibility. Self-authoring schools are often thoughtful places.

Educators are drawn together by a work vision, a common ethos and shared values. The decision-making process is value-oriented. The school engages in critical thinking and uses its core values as a touchstone. The self-authoring school is open to new ideas.

Self-authoring schools have a minimum of rules. Instead they have clearly understood expectations; such expectations focus on values, beliefs, and role clarity.

In self-authoring schools the pseudo-trust of collegial loyalty is replaced by what Bryk and Schneider (2005) call Relational Trust. Bryk and Schneider conducted their research in the Chicago school system and identified three kinds of social trust: organic, contractual, and relational.

Organic trust is based on faith and is the kind of trust that deeply religious people have in their church or temple, but is generally not appropriate for the fabric of school culture. Schools by definition are places where questioning, skepticism and critical thinking are welcomed. Organic trust may not support these activities.

Contractual trust is when we need to specify all the details of the relationship or agreement. Contractual trust is commonly found in the construction industry, where the contract will specify that the bathroom should have porcelain fixtures, not plastic ones. The last thing the homeowner wants at the completion of the project is an unpleasant surprise!

Not surprisingly, Bryk and Schneider found that contractual trust was not appropriate for the complex work of teachers in schools. The human relationships that form the environment of learning are far too complicated and changeable to be summed up in a bill of quantities.

The third form of trust, Bryk and Schneider labeled 'Relational'. This is the trust that becomes the glue that binds self-authoring schools together. Relational trust is based upon clearly understood roles and responsibilities (based, of course, on shared values and beliefs). As a teacher, I understand the different roles I undertake with respect to my students, their parents, and my colleagues. I understand my obligations in each of these relationships.

I also understand what I can reasonably expect from other stakeholders within the schoolhouse. Clarity of these obligations and expectations fall into four domains which Bryk and Schneider refer to as Criteria for Discernment: the yardsticks that we use to determine a person's or an organization's trustworthiness. The criteria for discernment include: respect, competence, personal regard for others, and integrity.

Teacher supervision in self-authoring schools combines a focus on teacher behavior and student learning. It is driven by a mutually-agreed set of standards. Feedback to teachers combines objective data with subjective observations (professional judgment on the part of the supervisor).

The focus on the supervision extends into areas that are not easily measured and quantified (How interesting is the teacher? How inspirational? What are the quality of the learning relationships within the classroom?) Teachers set professional goals for themselves and monitor their own progress towards meeting those goals. There is a degree of teacher self-assessment and there are pockets of reflective practice. Feedback to teachers tends to be primarily evaluative (commendations and recommendations), but does include data collection from multiple sources and descriptive comments. Sometimes protocols, such as Looking for Learning (Fieldwork, 2008) are implemented.

Adult professional growth is promoted, but the school may continue to be risk-averse. One quite mature school in Southeast Asia had a practice of not appointing principals or vice principals from within the ranks of the teaching faculty. The rationale was 'we are not a training ground for administrators'.

In self-authoring schools, professional learning is carefully designed to focus on student and school learning needs. There are strategic delimiters in place, which keep the organization focused on its learning goals. Professional learning is planned over a number of years, often with follow up peer coaching. Such professional learning includes study of theory, demonstrations, skill practice and on-going peer coaching.

As a result, there is some transfer from the workshop setting to classroom implementation. However, the impetus for professional learning still resides with the ascribed school leadership (director, principals). Professional learning is primarily informational, but can be transformational if the individual participant chooses to embrace it.

Self-authoring schools will often develop cultures of positive peer group pressure (both among students and teachers). Teachers will extend themselves far beyond what their contract requires because they take pride in their work and high quality products have become the group norm. The danger here is that such schools can become pressure-cookers for both students and teachers and stress can become debilitating.

When Bill was head of the International School of Kuala Lumpur, a newly elected board member asked him what time teachers finished work. Bill replied that classes finished just before three in the afternoon. No, the board member replied, "I mean when can teachers leave to go home?" Bill was stumped. The question had not been asked before.

Most teachers were in their classrooms until five or even six o'clock in the evening. Some returned in the evening to prepare, or answered student emails at home. Most weekends saw a very significant number of teachers on campus leading various sports, musical or theatrical activities. The board member's question was about accountability, but the school had already moved to responsibility.

There are, however, dangers that hover on the perimeters of self-authoring schools. The first is arrogance. In the first chapter, we describe the International School of the Andaman Sea that believed it was the best, or at least one of the best international schools in the world. When we internalize our values and beliefs and then act to realize them there is a natural tendency to take great pride in our accomplishments. That pride can easily result in blinkered vision and blind us to our shortcomings and alternative prospects. On occasion such arrogance takes on a quasi-divine quality. One head of a self-authoring school told us recently that his task was "to identify the inevitable, and then work backwards".

The second danger is that of 'silo thinking' (Collins, 2001). This is when the organization is fragmented into small groups that don't communicate with each other. The individual teams may be high functioning and collectively intelligent but may have lost sight of the roles and responsibilities within the larger organization.

Self-authoring schools often have ambitious strategic plans, the development of which can take a large number of people a long time. Strategic planning has become very fashionable and most self-authoring schools would be embarrassed to be caught without one. Some strategic plans may actually improve student learning, but in our experience many are not worth the immense effort that goes into their creation.

They either contain activities that would have to be done anyway (write a self-study for accreditation, refurbish the gym) or they confuse goals and strategies – a confusion most noticeable at the measurement stage of the process.

For example, the strategic goal might be the school-wide improvement of student writing. The strategies might include a workshop for teachers on process writing and the implementation of an annual standardized writing sample. Within twelve's months the two strategies have been implemented and there is the *assumption* that the goal has been achieved, but actually no one has attempted to measure whether student writing has improved. In the next section on self-transforming schools, we will explore scenario development as an alternative to strategic planning.

Duncan (2007) finds the idea of strategic planning wanting because it doesn't address where the ideas come from in the first place. Duncan asserts that we do not theorize the next creative idea, but rather we discover it through reflective practice and insight. We would add that this reflective practice is exponentially enhanced when it involves group knowledge processing.

Arie de Geus (1997), author of *The Living Company,* is decidedly disenchanted with strategic planning. He sees much of it as the futile quest for future certainty. He suggests that the word 'strategy' tends to be misused. 'It should not be a noun; you should not "have" a strategy –in the sense of a document the organization follows. Rather, "strategy" should be a verb: strategy is something you *do*, rather than something you *have*' (p155). The old adage from boxing comes to mind: 'Everyone has a strategy until they get hit.'

Self-authoring schools recognize that conflict is inevitable and, if managed well, is healthy. These schools understand and appreciate that conflict comes in two flavors: affective and cognitive. Affective conflict is personalized confrontation that is destructive to relationships and teamwork. It breeds suspicion, fear and mistrust and is characterized by name-calling, blaming, sarcasm and innuendo.

Cognitive conflict, on the other hand, focuses on issues and ideas. It is a respectful exchange and exploration of differing and alternative views with the goal of anticipating consequences and making the best possible decisions. Self-authoring schools do not attempt to avoid conflict or its resolution. They attempt to *manage* it. In other words, self-authoring schools attempt to keep the conflict in the cognitive domain.

Strategies for keeping conflict cognitive include active, reflective and respectful listening, the seven norms of collaboration, and developing the ethos of a loyal opposition (the devil's advocate) – we don't shoot the messenger bringing the bad news, we thank him.

Self-authoring schools understand that quality control can never be imposed in a learning organization. It can't be installed through complicated appraisal or inspection systems. Self-authoring schools manage the delicate balance between accountability interventions and capacity building. Leaders in self-authoring schools delegate *both* the responsibility and the authority.

What supports and challenges serve the self-authoring school? Self-authoring groups are often self-reliant and self-directed. While they need psychological safety and encouragement, they often thrive on delegation. Many such groups are high on efficacy, but may lack consciousness and flexibility.

In other words, they may have very clear goals and feel empowered to achieve them, but may not appreciate how the goals fit into the larger scheme of the school as a whole. Mediative questions that probe into interdependence may prove a useful challenge. The efficacy and enthusiasm that such groups may feel may actually blind them to alternative ways of realizing their goals.

In addition, while self-authoring schools have internalized values and beliefs, they still may be in the process of developing collective emotional intelligence. Reflection activities that focus on social sensitivity may also be very useful. Self-authoring groups can also enhance their collective intelligence by training in both facilitation and coaching skills.

Self-transforming schools

Self-transforming schools are very rare. In 35 years of working with schools, we have only encountered three. Probably the most significant difference between a self-authoring school and self-transforming school has to do with knowledge. Self-authoring schools consume knowledge. Self-transforming schools generate knowledge. They are truly 'lab schools', where new ideas are regularly generated and scrutinized and where experimentation and field-testing are the norm. Innovation is valued and shared. There is a culture of professional excitement. Colleagues visit each other's classes to see works in progress; action research is common and teachers regularly contribute to professional publications.

In self-transforming schools authority and democracy blend seamlessly into a sense of higher moral purpose. Leadership is distributed and there is enough collective emotional intelligence to understand that 'being right isn't a strategy'. (Fullan 2011, p41)

Self-transforming schools believe their mission is larger than mere organizational self. Self-transforming schools assume a leadership responsibility for teaching and learning that extends beyond its own borders. We saw this phenomenon in the 1960s when the International School of Geneva and the United Nations International School in New York embarked on developing what in future years would become the International Baccalaureate Programme. We saw it when a group of international schools leaders got together to design the International Primary School Curriculum Project, later to become the IB PYP.

A self-transforming school is a purposeful work community that is future focused. There is a great deal of structured inquiry and reflection, and frequent examination of assumptions and perceptions. Most stakeholders (teachers, administrators, students and even parents) perceive themselves as learners and are eager to understand the perceptions and assumptions of others. There is a great deal of dialogue, and, as a result, creativity is a regular feature of meetings.

Self-transforming schools often pursue contradictory goals. This is not an easy road, but the complexity of high organizational intelligence demands it. For example, maintaining a simultaneous focus on quality control in schools (teacher supervision) and promoting teacher empowerment may at first blush appear contradictory, but upon further examination are complementary.

Another often perceived contradiction in terms of school goals is the simultaneous pursuit of curricular standards and instructional differentiation. Self-transforming schools not only tolerate, but embrace such ambiguity.

Teacher supervision in self-transforming schools is differentiated to meet the developmental needs of the individuals. There may be different levels of supervision that correspond to the experience, expertise and self-directedness of the individual concerned. For example, some schools have supervisory stages that include Probationary (the teacher is ineffective and is working on an improvement plan); Direct (the teacher is new to the school and is regularly observed by the supervisor); Transitional (teacher takes responsibility for own professional learning, sets goals and self-assesses); and Leadership (the individual takes responsibility for own professional learning and contributes actively to the professional learning of colleagues).

What makes differentiated supervision self-transforming is the explicit expectation that virtually every teacher in the school must achieve transitional or leadership levels of supervision within 18 months. Self-transforming schools are communities of self-directed individuals who work on common goals.

The premise behind differentiated teacher supervision is that of a developmental stance: leadership provides appropriate supports (psychological safety, encouragement *etc*) and challenges (stretch goals). In a self-transforming school everyone has a 'good problem' that he or she is working on. Feedback is much less evaluative.

Self-transforming schools understand that there are two major myths surrounding evaluative feedback. The first is that feedback helps people to see themselves more accurately. The second is that feedback improves team effectiveness. The contrary is true in both cases (Sanford 1995). In self-transforming schools feedback is often neutral data combined with a mediative or reflective question. Garmston concludes that evaluative feedback actually reduces the capabilities of self-reflection and self-assessment by reinforcing the pattern and expectation that others will and should tell us how we are doing (2012, p125).

Professional learning in self-transforming schools is embedded in the daily work environment. It is not something extra that happens on weekends or during the summer holidays. Every day is a learning day. Colleagues feel comfortable talking about what and how they are learning. It can include informational learning, but is primarily transformational in that both individuals and the organization connect the new insights and ideas to their values, beliefs and identity.

Self-transforming schools have high degrees of relational trust. There is a great deal of social capital; good faith and positive presumptions are the norm. In self-transforming schools with enhanced collective intelligence, self-conscious attention is regularly paid to the four attributes of relational trust: respect, competence, personal regard for others, and integrity. These are not passive 'givens', but rather pressing outcomes to be achieved on a daily basis. There is probably no more important task for school leaders than to build a fabric of relational trust within schools.

Self-transforming schools are often masterful at keeping conflict in the cognitive domain. They need to be because they are centers of innovation and educational leadership. They are also able to distinguish between solving problems and managing polarities. There is a subtle but important difference here. Problems can be solved by a right answer or a series of right answers. A problem might be: what are we going to do about the overcrowded staff car park? The solutions might include expansion and/or carpooling.

Polarities, on the other hand, are problems without solutions, because the solution, as with the oscillating systems that we looked at earlier, would create a new problem even more serious that the previous one. Polarities are tensions between mutually desirable entities. Garmston writes: 'Polarities to be managed are sets of opposites that can't function well independently. They require *both/and* thinking. Because the two sides of a polarity are interdependent, you cannot choose one as a solution and neglect the other' (Garmston 2012, p112).

The classic example of polarities in schools is the inevitable tension between the business manager and the principal. The principal wants to spend money to purchase resources that will improve student learning. The business manager wants to conserve finances, stay within budget, and build reserves. The tension is necessary. If either side is perceived to be the 'solution', the school could be in deep trouble. Polarity management involves unpacking the interrelated and healthy relationships between the polarities.

Developmental stages of schools

	Instrumental	Socializing	Self-authoring	Self-transforming
Mission— school values and beliefs	Mission is not stated or does not in any way reflect actual practice. Teachers are often in survival mode.	Mission is shared by the few who wrote/endorsed it. Values may come from external sources and may not be widely shared by stakeholders.	School mission is developed collaboratively among stakeholders and guides decision-making and resource allocation.	Stakeholders select the school because of its mission. Values drive daily decision-making. Stakeholders take pride in shared norms and values.
School culture	Little trust is expected. Contractual trust is often a source of conflict.	Pseudo-trust is present: there is a sense of collegial loyalty and conviviality.	Relational trust is present. Expectations and role obligations are mostly clear.	Teachers seek out opportunities to establish, maintain and celebrate the fabric of relational trust.
Strategic planning	If there is a long term plan, it is often dictated from external sources (accreditation agencies, central office, *eg* raise standardized test scores).	There is some long term planning often reflecting trends in other schools. Common practice is seen as best practice.	The strategic plan reflects the values and beliefs of the organization. There may be confusion between goals and strategies. The strategic plan may also be overwhelming.	The school engages in scenario planning. Goals are broad and clearly stated. Strategies are fluid and flexible.
Professional learning	Little or none. Prevailing belief is that once teachers are qualified, they are finished products. PD may be perceived as implied criticism.	Some professional learning reflecting educational fads. PD is not coherent. Teachers do not see connections and may be overwhelmed.	A considerable amount of professional learning is taking place. It is coherent and coordinated. Teachers see connections, but most is informational learning. It is usually separate from daily craft practice, (*eg* workshops or conferences).	Professional learning is integrated in everyday practice. There is a great deal of original action research. There is a great deal of transformational learning.

Approaches to teacher supervision	One size fits all checklist evaluations. Teachers ranked according to student test scores.	One size fits all checklist evaluations that are used to "encourage" teachers. Little meaningful descriptive feedback.	Supervision focuses on both teacher behavior and student learning. Some descriptive feedback and individual teacher goal setting.	Differentiated supervision. Teachers receive data and reflective questions and are expected to self-assess and set goals. Teacher self-direction is expected and encouraged.
Approaches to handling conflict	Use of power. Conflict resolution often produces winners and losers.	Conflict avoidance. Teams do not distinguish between cognitive and affective conflict	Teachers consciously attempt to keep conflict in cognitive domain.	Conflict kept in cognitive domain. Polarity management is present. Inquiry is placed at the center

We began the description of different levels of organizational development by stating that there are probably no pure types. Schools are organic and their development is in a constant state of flux. Nevertheless, teachers and schools leaders who foster a 'developmental stance' can become the architects of organizational growth and enhanced collective intelligence.

Guiding study questions

When you think about your present school, what evidence do you see of the various developmental stages?

The authors state that one of the most important responsibilities of teachers and school leaders is to establish and maintain a school culture of relational trust. What are some practical activities that teachers can engage in that further relational trust?

Given a primarily socializing team of teachers, what are some supports and challenges that would facilitate collective growth?

How might a self-authoring school define student success?

Write a brief mission statement for a self-transforming school.

Looking beneath the surface activity

One way to develop a group's flexibility of thought is to engage in an activity that requires the group to analyze and explore assumptions that may lie beneath the surface of everyday expressions and their implications. This analysis can support groups in recognizing false but commonly held dichotomies and the influence of frequently-used metaphors on our decision-making and behavior.

The facilitator collects a series of collegial expressions, newspaper headlines or advertisements that might need 'uncoverage' (deep analysis) and the group then analyzes them for the assumptions upon which they are based and the implications of those assumptions. Some examples of expressions worthy of analysis:

"If it isn't broken, don't fix it."

"Leadership is a human right."

"Live free or die."

"People are successful or not because of their achievements."

"An agnostic is a cowardly atheist."

"A phonemic approach to learning to read inhibits a love of literature."

"In a class that culminates in an external examination, teachers have to cover content; they don't have time for differentiated learning."

"Freedom of speech is an inalienable right."

"The just war justifies too much."

Squaring the circle activity

Squaring the circle is an activity that illustrates how groups self-organize and move from chaos to intelligent order. It also provides an opportunity for groups to reflect on how leadership and systems thinking emerge, analyze how group dynamics play out, and identify strategies that lead to effective problem solving.

Participants: 15-40. If you have between 10-15, we may wish to triangle the circle.

Time: approximately 30 minutes.

Materials: one length of rope, 15 meters or longer, depending upon the size of the group.

Directions: the facilitator will need a length of rope (approximately one meter for each participant).

Participants form a single line, shoulder to shoulder, facing the facilitator and hold their hands outstretched, palms up. The facilitator places the end of the rope in the hands of the person at the end of the line and walks down the line placing the rope into the hands of each participant. When the facilitator reaches the end of the line, s/he walks back to the first person, playing out the rope on the floor, and then ties the two ends of the rope together. At this point the participants are bunched on one half of the loop. The facilitator then tells the participants:

The entire rope must be used.

Close your eyes and keep them closed during the entire activity.

You may slide along the rope, but you cannot change positions with anyone else on the rope.

When you think the group is finished with the task, raise your hand and the facilitator will call for a vote.

If a majority of the group thinks the task is finished, the facilitator will ask you to stop, open your eyes and lay the rope on the floor. Otherwise s/he will tell you to keep going.

Your goal is to create a perfect square while everyone maintains his or her hold on the rope.

After the group finishes the task, the facilitator conducts a debriefing. Questions might include:

What happened during the first few minutes of the activity?

How does this compare with the minutes at the end of the activity?

How effective was the group's communication?

What strategies emerged?

How were the strategies communicated?

In what ways did leadership emerge?

In what ways did the group achieve enhanced collective intelligence?

The museum tour activity

The museum tour activity works well when a group is attempting to synthesize and process new learning. It challenges groups to be creative and imaginative. It explicitly supports team members in making connections and achieving new insights. The museum tour works best in groups of between five and eight members and takes roughly 45 minutes to an hour.

Step one: Give each team member five index cards and ask him or her to write on each card a single word or phrase that captures a key idea of the new learning. For example, if the topic was personalized learning, the words or phrases might include 'reflection', 'self-discovery', 'strategies', 'knowing our students', 'student choice', 'production style preferences', 'empathy', and 'conceptual teaching'.

Step two: Ask team members to share their cards with the table group and to organize the cards into four or five meaningful categories. Don't rush this stage as it is often here that new connections are made.

Step three: Instruct the group to build a three-dimensional metaphor that represents their collective thinking about the concept or topic. They can use whatever building material they so choose (it is helpful to have a supply of lollipop sticks, string, ribbon, masking tape *etc* on hand), but they also have to use all the cards.

Step four: As the construction of the metaphor nears completion, instruct each group to appoint a docent – a guide who will make a brief (90 second) presentation on the metaphor. Better yet, if you have multiple groups, 'jigsaw' the groups so that every team member has to make the presentation.

Chapter 9

Measuring and growing our OIQ factor

Measuring and growing are not the same things. The distinction in fields other than education is often straightforward. We can easily see the difference between measuring our harvest of corn or wheat and the process of fertilizing and irrigating our fields. But measurement and growth are often confused in education.

Teachers may sometimes believe that by giving a weekly spelling quiz, they are teaching children to spell. Likewise, pundits in government ministries assume that standardized testing will result in improved classroom learning. As a Yorkshire farmer once said, "you don't fatten a cow by weighing it."

But there are important connections between measurement and growth. When we carefully measure something over time, we can analyze the conditions under which growth has taken place and strive to identify the factors and conditions that contribute to it.

Why should measurement in education be both so important and so problematic? Simply put, measurement is one of the primary ways that we order and attempt to make meaning out of the world around us. Measurement is the canvas upon which achievement is realized and recorded; it is in the background of the goals we set for ourselves; it lies at the heart of self-assessment, motivation and future learning. And yet, when we attempt to measure things that are not easily quantified, we are notoriously bad at it.

So what are some of the factors that make a group more intelligent? The answers provided by recent research may surprise you. In this chapter we will explore some ways in which schools can measure and grow their collective intelligence.

There have been recent attempts at both defining and measuring collective intelligence. Malone, Woolley and colleagues (2010) from MIT's Sloan School of Management have conducted research in order to test the hypothesis that groups, like individuals, do have characteristic levels of intelligence that can be measured and used to predict the group's performance on a variety of challenging tasks.

In one study, researchers had 40 three-person groups working together for five hours on a variety of tasks that included solving visual puzzles, brainstorming, making collective moral judgments and negotiating over limited resources. Before the start of the session, the researchers measured the individual intelligence of each team member.

The findings support the hypothesis that collective intelligence (which they labeled 'c') does in fact exist in groups, but more interestingly is not significantly correlated with the average and maximum intelligence scores of the individual group members. In other words smart individuals, when brought together into a group, don't necessarily demonstrate a high degree of collective intelligence. The results demonstrate that collective intelligence is the property of the group itself, not just the composition of the individuals in it (Woolley *et al*, 2010).

The researchers then went on to examine factors that one might have expected would influence collective intelligence (group performance) including group cohesion, motivation, and satisfaction. They found that these were *not* statistically significantly correlated to collective intelligence.

They did, however, find three factors that were significantly correlated with group intelligence: the average social sensitivity of the group members; the equal distribution of conversational turn-taking; and the number of females in the group. Let's examine each of these in turn.

According to their results, groups that included socially-sensitive and perceptive individuals were more collectively intelligent. The researchers measured the social sensitivity of individual members by using the Reading the Mind in the Eyes test (Baron-Cohen, 2003), which asks the participants to identify emotions such as fear, anger, and joy that may be represented in photographs in which all facial features are masked other than the eyes.

This test does not call for deliberate cognition. In fact, in our experience the more one 'thinks' about the emotions that may be represented, the poorer one's overall score. The test measures the spontaneous, non-verbal, social and emotional acuity of the individual (judgments that are made without conscious thought). And yet the accuracy of these judgments was significantly correlated to the enhanced group cognition.

The second factor that was significantly correlated to enhanced collective intelligence was conversational turn taking. In other words, groups in which the conversation was dominated by a few individuals were less collectively intelligent than those with a more equal distribution of conversational turn taking. We can frame several questions from this finding.

First, did the more equal conversational turn-taking result in more ideas on the table? Did these ideas give the groups more avenues to explore? Secondly, did the more equal conversational turn-taking represent a higher degree of collective trust? (Silent group members are frequently those who feel either a degree of anxiety and intimidation, a sense of being dismissed by other group members or simply a lack of belonging and membership to the group.) And third, does the more equal conversational turn-taking suggest that there was more active and reflective listening on the part of the individual members?

The third factor that enhanced collective intelligence was the number of females in the group. Yes, you read that correctly. Statistically speaking, the more women in the group the smarter the group. The researchers were quick to point out that this was not related to a diversity factor – in other words, there was no point of diminishing returns. There was simply a linear progression: the more women, the smarter the group.

While individually there is no statistically-significant difference in the IQ of men and women, there was a significant difference when it came to group work. The researchers speculate that this may be because, on average, women tend to score higher than men on tests of social sensitivity – a factor positively correlated to group intelligence.

Organizational intelligence in schools:
The macro and micro picture

As we stated earlier, measurement and planning for growth are inter-related and, in order to understand the relationship when it comes to developing enhanced organizational intelligence, we need to look at both the macro and micro picture of the school. The macro view allows us a holistic assessment of the organization, but doesn't chart a course for growth. The micro picture examines specific behaviors that we can self-consciously develop that will contribute to enhanced collective intelligence.

Let's start by examining the macro picture. Let's identify some of the traits of schools with high degrees of organizational intelligence. These tend to be schools that:

Engage in visioning

These are future-oriented schools that are actively translating their commonly shared beliefs and values into planning for their preferred future. These schools are thoughtful, inclusive, proactive and adaptive.

These are schools that clearly distinguish between goals and strategies; come to recognize our collective identity as a work in progress; and accept that knowledge is tentative and assumptions are ephemeral. These are schools with collective growth mindsets that are not inhibited by uncertainty. These are schools that delight in the process of becoming.

Manage holonomy

The word 'holonomy' was coined by the writer and social critic Arthur Koestler (1967) and represents the tension that we feel between two polarities: our need to be autonomous individuals, captains of our destiny, architects of our future AND our simultaneous need to be part of something larger than ourselves – a family, a friendship group, a collegial faculty.

Schools that have high degrees of collective intelligence tolerate, appreciate and manage this tension. They celebrate individual accomplishment and nurture collective creativity and innovation. In these schools there is a strong sense of *esprit de corps*, a strong sense of shared fate, but never at the expense of the individual.

Increase our appetite for change

These are schools in which educators recognize that school improvement is not an option, but an imperative. There is no such thing as the *status quo*. Schools are either improving or deteriorating.

Engage in prosocial activities

Prosocial activity is any voluntary behavior that is intended to benefit another person or persons such as donating, sharing, helping, co-operating and volunteering. Prosocial behavior requires discretionary effort. In other words, teachers who engage in such behavior do so out of personal choice and not contractual obligation. Examples might include: teachers voluntarily serving on committees, offering extra-curricular activities, additional homework assistance, attending evening events at school or engaging in community service projects.

Have structural congruence

There is role clarity in that stakeholders understand what is expected of them and what they can expect from others. Norms, patterns of behavior and clearly understood expectations and obligations keep individuals and groups from stepping on each other's toes. Such structural congruence is the foundation of relational trust.

Internalized performance pressure

Motivation to perform well comes from within the individual and the group. There is a positive peer group pressure that propels both teachers and students to achieve. We used to think that passion and motivation drive accomplishment but Fullan (2011) argues that the inverse is also true: one of the strongest drivers of school improvement is the *accomplishment* of something with high moral value.

Knowledge is shared

There is an open source approach to craft knowledge. Individuals and groups celebrate each others' capacity to create, share and apply knowledge. There is an openness about who we can learn from.

A rubric for organizational intelligence

Dimensions of OIQ/ levels of development	Rudimentary	Emerging	Developing	Advancing
Leadership	Autocratic, frequent command-decisions. Little or no consultation.	Socializing, a great deal of consultation. Many committees, labor intensive, but probably not very productive.	Authoritative, solution-centered leadership. Driven by expertise and experience. Values and beliefs are leadership / decision –making touchstones.	Distributed, inquiry-centered leadership. There is a developmental stance. Individuals are provided appropriate supports and challenges.
Professional relationships	Teachers are isolated and tend to work on their own. Sharing craft knowledge is not the norm and requests for help may be greeted by resentment or derision. The need to learn may be viewed as an admission of weakness.	Professional relationships are characterized by conviviality. There is a pleasant feeling about the school. However, there is little collaboration or collective learning.	The school is actively trying to develop professional learning communities. Time is set aside for teacher collaboration and reflection, but teachers may lack the skills and understandings.	Teachers are provided with necessary training in collaboration and reflection. Coaching and mentoring is part of daily life. Leadership learns publicly and encourages others to do so.
Professional motivation	External – rewards and punishments.	Approval of supervisors and peers.	Fulfillment of internal values and beliefs.	Pursuit of understanding and wisdom. Widespread participation in school committees.
Prosocial activities	Few or none. Union contract may actually prohibit prosocial behavior.	Some teacher participation but these are individual decisions, unrelated to the school.	School has a program of community service and both students and teachers are encouraged to participate.	Widespread volunteerism. Teachers get a great sense of satisfaction in going beyond what is contractually required.

Knowledge deployment	Craft knowledge held within the individual. What little sharing there is happens coincidentally.	Some sharing of craft knowledge, but no systematic opportunities for personal growth	Knowledge is shared and structures are in place to support such sharing. Knowledge is used	Knowledge is not only shared, but is generated. Action research is encouraged and teachers are perceived as researchers.
School culture	Often toxic. Fear and anxiety present. Rumor and gossip are rife.	Purpose of school is to provide teachers with employment. Student learning is a desirable by-product.	Deeply held values and beliefs are identified and are used in decision making when other factors (eg vested self-interest) don't interfere.	School's mission is clearly understood and individuals and groups use it as a touchstone for decision making and daily work. Values and beliefs inspire and energize.

The micro picture:
measuring and enhancing the way we work together

Bob Garmston (2009) is fond of saying that any group that is too busy to reflect on *how* its members are working together is a group that is too busy to improve. Implicit in the statement is the recognition that process effects productivity (if it doesn't, then the task could probably be accomplished better and more efficiently by individuals working in isolation). The relatively short amount of time given over to reflecting on our work together can pay tremendous dividends.

One headmaster in the Middle East met weekly with the nine-member leadership team. Once every five or six weeks, the last 10-15 minutes of the meeting would be reserved for an inventory of the seven norms of collaboration (see page 177).

Individuals would use the inventory form to evaluate their contribution to the group knowledge processing and how they felt the group was doing as a whole. Each individual would report out to the group and there would follow a conversation during which the group would prioritize the norm or norms that the team would work on for the following month.

The inventory process engaged the team in measuring group effectiveness on the micro level and in short term goals setting (growing our collective intelligence). A major premise here is that organizational transformation happens concurrently with individual transformations (Rooke & Torbet, 2005). What follows is a copy of the inventory that the leadership team at ISKL used. This is adapted from the work of Bob Garmston and Bruce Wellman in *The Adaptive School: Facilitating Collaborative Groups* (2009).

Norms of collaboration inventory
Self-evaluation for individuals and for the team
1: Behavior is absent 3:Behavior is present sporadically 5: Behavior is used frequently

	Myself					The group				
NORMS	1	2	3	4	5	1	2	3	4	5
Pausing:										
I/We pause after asking a question.										
I/We pause after others speak.										
I/We pause after responding.										
Paraphrasing:										
I/We paraphrase to acknowledge and clarify.										
I/We paraphrase to organize and summarize.										
I/We paraphrase to shift levels of abstraction.										
Probing:										
I/We seek to understand the meaning of unfamiliar or ambiguous words/phrases.										
I/We seek to understand the meaning of data, explanations, ideas and generalizations.										
I/We seek to understand assumptions and perceptions and their implications.										
Putting inquiry at the center:										
I/We inquire in order to explore perceptions and assumptions.										

I/We invite others to inquire into my/our perceptions and assumptions.										
I/We inquire before engaging in advocacy.										
Putting ideas on the table:										
I/We state the intention of my/our communication.										
I/We present relevant facts, ideas opinions and inferences.										
I/We announce modifications of ideas or points of view.										
I/We remove weak ideas from consideration.										
Paying attention to self and others:										
I/We balance participation and open opportunities for others to contribute.										
I/We regulate impulses to react and respond at inappropriate times or in ineffective ways.										
I/We maintain an awareness of the group's task, processes, and overall development.										
I/We explicitly identify the effective use of norms of collaboration										
Presuming positive intentions:										
I/We communicate respectfully whether I agree or disagree.										
I/We suspend judgment until the issues are well understood.										
I/We embed positive presuppositions in my paraphrases, questions and comments.										

The micro picture feedback:
The breakfast of champions and losers

One of the most telling features of schools with a high degree of organizational intelligence is the formation and use of meaningful feedback. Recent research (Hattie 2012, Wiliam 2012) is suggesting a very strong correlation between effective feedback and student learning. Not surprisingly, effective feedback is also directly correlated to organizational intelligence and the group learning.

For over 75 years, the American breakfast cereal manufacturer Wheaties has advertised its product as the 'breakfast of champions' – clearly trying to forge connections in the consumer's mind between exemplary performance and their product.

In education, researchers and teachers have also been searching for the 'breakfast of champions' and we have found one; the only down side – and it is a very significant one – is that our 'breakfast' can produce both champions and losers. Feedback can be a double-edged sword.

When Hattie (2010) ranked the statistical influences on student learning, feedback was number ten out of more than 135. However, when researchers Kluger and DeNisi (1996) analyzed 131 carefully constructed studies of teacher feedback, they found that while feedback did on average improve student learning, in over 40% of the research studies feedback actually made student performance *worse!* Thus feedback is both the breakfast of champions and losers. Feedback also has a powerful influence of collective intelligence and group effectiveness.

Dylan Wiliam (2012) points out that there are several ways that individuals can respond to feedback: by changing behavior (increasing* or decreasing effort); by modifying a goal (reducing or increasing* level of challenge); by abandoning the goal (deciding that the goal is too easy or too difficult); or by rejecting the feedback (ignoring the feedback). Six out of the eight responses have a *negative* impact on future learning. The positive responses are indicated with an asterisk. While Wiliam was writing about individual learning, the same is true for groups.

It is incumbent on those concerned with teaching and learning to become feedback literate.

Feedback literacy

Simply defined, feedback is information about how an individual or group is doing in their efforts to reach a goal. In order for the feedback to be meaningful, the goal must be clearly understood. In other words the learning target, task or problem to be solved must be clear. The acid test is to ask every member of the group to individually complete the sentence stem: *Our goal is...* The results can be both surprising and informative.

In order for feedback to be both effective and meaningful, the group needs to be able to answer three metacognitive questions that are deceptively simple and yet powerfully reflective: Where are we going? (What is the learning target or group goal?) Where are we now? (What is our present level of understanding?) and How do we close the gap? (Chappius 2005).

Two flavors of misunderstanding

There are two very common teacher misunderstandings about feedback. The first is that evaluative comments in and of themselves constitute useful feedback. Nothing could be further from the truth. Such comments tell individuals and groups nothing specific about how they have performed or what they need to do next in terms of improvement. In fact, often such evaluative comments signal that a task or project is finished and can be filed away. No further thought is required.

The second is that the responsibility of the author of the feedback ends with providing feedback; and that it is the recipient's responsibility to use it. Teachers are often much better at providing feedback than they are at ensuring students use it. Giving feedback that isn't acted upon is arguably the single most wasteful use of teacher time!

In short, the acid test of effective feedback is the response of the recipient. Everyone, students and adults alike, makes decisions about who we will learn from. Teachers develop positive relationships with colleagues and informal and formal mentoring takes place. The same thing happens in the classroom. We learn much more effectively and efficiently from people we are comfortable with. Feedback is much more likely to be well-received from someone we trust. Teachers need to deliberately and proactively develop climates of classroom trust and groups need to actively foster climates of trust.

Feedback flourishes when we encounter misunderstandings, misconceptions and errors. (When students understand and produce error-free work, feedback is generally ineffective in terms of promoting future learning). Adult teams need to create a climate in which error and misunderstandings are welcome. Failure is not something to hide or be ashamed of.

Outside education there is a clear understanding that creativity and innovation are directly correlated to the degree to which we fail. We are reminded of the provocative statement about the relationship between failure and innovation: if we are not failing nine times out of ten, we are not taking enough risks (Sawyer, 2007). Keith Sawyer exhorts us: 'Fail frequently, fail early (recognize failure early and don't throw good money/ time after bad) and fail gloriously!' (p178)

Whether we are supporting the learning of students in the classroom or colleagues in team meetings, our feedback needs to focus on errors and not mistakes. What is the difference? Mistakes are the result of a temporary lapse of attention. When we are exhausted or distracted and our mind wanders from the task at hand, we will often make mistakes.

We often catch mistakes ourselves or recognize them quickly when others point them out. We know what we have done wrong and we know how to correct them. Teachers shouldn't spend a lot of time giving students feedback on mistakes.

What we should focus on is errors. Errors result from either a lack of knowledge or a misunderstanding. Even when an error is pointed out to a student, he or she may not know what to do about it. As Fisher and Frey (2012) write: 'Correcting mistakes while failing to address errors can be a costly waste of instructional time.' (p44)

Comfort-oriented feedback

Perhaps the most insidious form of feedback is comfort-oriented feedback. Four recent studies indicate that comforting students who struggle in math de-motivate them and decrease the number of students pursuing math-related subjects (Rattan, Good & Dweck, 2012).

While these studies focused on math, our experience suggests that the findings are transferable to a host of different situations. These studies explored whether holding a fixed theory of ability – that is believing that ability is innate and unchanging – leads teachers and parents not only to comfort students for their perceived low ability following failure, but also to use practices that actually encourage student long-term low achievement.

The studies found that teachers and parents who have a fixed theory of math intelligence more frequently judged students to have low ability in math than those who held a malleable theory, which supposes that people can improve their abilities through hard work and practice. They were also more likely to comfort students for their apparent lack of ability and use 'kind' strategies that failed to motivate the student to improve, such as assigning less homework and not calling on them in class.

Students who received comfort-oriented feedback often assumed the teacher had low expectations for what they might accomplish as well as lower engagement in their learning even when the feedback was expressed positively – as in "You are a good person who has many talents. It may be that you just don't have an aptitude for learning a foreign language."

The report concluded that teachers and parents who provided comfort-oriented feedback might have done so with the best of intentions. These may be exceptionally kind and empathetic teachers, but they inadvertently disable students from future learning.

We find a similar situation in collegial relationships. When a teacher describes the difficulties she may be encountering with a specific student and a colleague attempts to comfort her by saying something like: "There'll always be some kids who just don't get it. I had Jimmy last year and I didn't do any better with him. Look at his home life. He comes from a totally dysfunctional family."

In order to provide truly effective feedback, we have to understand our intentions and choose congruent behavior. Feedback can be used to promote a variety of responses in the people who receive it. These can include compliance, conformity, informing about best practice, giving advice, expressing opinions and promoting self-directed learning – the last being the hallmark of mature and intelligent groups.

The table below illustrates the different intentions, purposes and possible reactions of six different kinds of feedback. It is often useful for teams to reflect on the types of feedback they are providing and to determine whether it matches with their intentions.

Types of feedback	Example	Support function	Purpose or intention	Analysis & cognition	Possible types of learning
Judgments	"You did a great job introducing the novel Moby Dick."	Evaluation	Compliance and conformity –quality control. Praise and criticism may be used to reinforce positive or modify negative behaviors.	External to the person receiving the feedback.	If evaluation is accepted, the learning will probably be informational (eg at the level of behaviors often with very limited transfer to classroom practice).
Personal advice or recommendations	"I think you should write your learning objectives on the white board."	Implicit evaluation/ explicit consultation.	Improving instruction, sharing expertise and experience.	External to the person receiving the feedback.	If advice or recommendation is accepted, the learning will probably be informational (at the level of behaviors or capabilities often with limited or temporary transfer to classroom practice).
Inferences	"The students were having fun, but they didn't understand the purpose of your lesson."	Evaluation/ consultation. The supervisor or colleague cannot actually observe 'fun' or the absence of 'understanding', but can infer them. The inference may or may not be accurate.	Improving instruction, sharing expertise and experience..	External to the person receiving the feedback.	If the inference is positive, it will be accepted as praise and little or no learning will take place. If the inference is received as criticism, it may well be rejected as "that's only your opinion." No data to support statement..
Data	"You spoke to eight students 1:1; you didn't speak to five students."	Coaching: providing neutral observable data so that the recipient can do the analysis.	Supporting the self-directed learning of the recipient.	Internal to the person receiving the feedback.	Data are neutral and meaningless. Therefore data are difficult to reject. The meaning of data comes from the analysis. This is most powerful when conducted by the recipient.

Reflective questions	"Given your interaction with students (see 'data' above) what decisions did you make about who you would speak to directly?"	Coaching: the combination of presenting data and a reflective question can encourage deep thinking, new insights, and new learnings.	Supporting the self-directed learning of the recipient.	Internal to the person receiving the feedback.	Transformational learning in that the new insights, connections and learnings often take place at the level of beliefs, values, mission and identity.
Comfort-oriented Feedback	"You mustn't blame yourself. I had Jimmy in my class last year. Math just isn't his thing – and look at the dysfunctional family he comes from."	Evaluation. Implicit in the statement is a lower expectation for student and teacher performance.	To make the recipient feel better.	Little or no analysis.	Comfort-oriented feedback may promote learned helplessness.

Conclusion

In order to make schools smarter collectively, we need to pay attention to both the background and the foreground, the broad landscape and the topographical details, the macro and the micro-picture.

Research on organizational intelligence is clear on three issues. First that the social sensitivity and perceptiveness of individual members enhance collective intelligence and such social sensitivity can be developed over time (Powell & Kusuma-Powell, 2010). Secondly, how we go about working together has a critical influence on our collective smarts, our creativity and innovation, and our wise decision-making. Thirdly, the feedback we offer and in turn receive serves as a remarkably accurate barometer of collective learning and organizational intelligence.

Chapter 10

Bringing it all together

We work in up to 35 schools in the course of a school year. They range from small schools in relatively isolated locations (sub-Saharan Africa to the outer islands of the Philippines) to very large schools in cosmopolitan centers (Singapore, San Francisco, Sao Paulo, Moscow etc.). Almost without exception, we hear from these schools a common refrain in terms of the challenges they face.

The challenges schools face

There are seven broad challenges facing schools around the world. These include:

Developing challenging, well-articulated, standards-based curricula (unit planning, vertical articulation, curriculum mapping, assessment and reporting); including 'learning to learn' or metacognition.

Developing highly skilled, creative and responsive teachers capable of meeting the increasingly diverse needs of students (differentiation/personalized learning).

Developing professional learning communities (de-privatizing teaching practice and reflection on practice).

Developing collaborative teams (common unit planning, co-teaching, collaborative analysis of student work, and reflection).

Promoting staff motivation (group identity and efficacy).

Managing change.

Managing time and tasks (prioritizing what really matters).

These are worthwhile, complex and meaningful challenges that schools need to address. What makes them truly complex is that each involves *both* technical and adaptive challenges. In other words, addressing these challenges in a meaningful way means engaging in both informational and transformational learning – learning that effects not just behavior and capabilities, but also addresses values, beliefs, assumptions, identity and our mission as educators.

This is difficult work that no individual should be asked to engage in on his or her own. They are challenges that must be addressed collectively in groups or teams, the effectiveness of which depends on the quality of relationships. Too often the quality of those relationships is left to chance. As a result, organizational intelligence or collective stupidity is a product of accident or chance. We can do better than this. High quality relationships can be developed by design.

One of our favorite educational writers, Roland Barth (2006), Professor Emeritus at Harvard, puts in succinctly: 'One incontrovertible finding emerges from my career spent in working in and around schools: the nature of relationships among adults within a school has a greater influence on the character and quality of that school and on student accomplishment than anything else.' (p8)

In his classic work *Improving Schools from Within* (1990), Barth states that within an hour or so of visiting a school and watching the adult-to-adult relationships he can arrive at a remarkably accurate judgment of the quality of student learning that is going on in the classroom. He suggests that there are four distinct types of professional relationships that are found in schools: parallel play; adversarial relationships; congenial relationships; and collegial relationships.

Parallel play, as the label suggests, happens when teachers work in isolation from each other and there is seldom any meaningful professional interaction. Teachers tend to be self-absorbed, working in self-contained classrooms with the door shut and construction paper pasted over the ubiquitous window in the door.

Adversarial relationships are surprisingly common in schools around the world and are manifest in a number of different ways. They can develop as an Us/Them relationship between the teachers and the school leadership team or they can be based on a culture of competition between teachers (*eg* "the worse you look, the better I look.")

Congenial relationships are characterized by positive and pleasant interactions. There are personal and friendly relationships that are often centered around food. However, the interactions rarely focus on professional matters.

Collegial relationships, as defined by Barth, have four characteristics:

Teachers talk to one another about their practice.

Teachers share craft knowledge with one another.

Teachers observe each other while engaged in practice.

Teachers celebrate each other's success.

Collegial relationships rarely happen by default. They are developed over time by conscious attention to relationship management and emotional intelligence. Druskat and Wolff (2001) suggest that such team effectiveness is predicated on three conditions: trust among members, a sense of group identity, and a sense of group efficacy. These characteristics can be developed by design – by deliberately and explicitly creating and maintaining group norms.

Norms, as stated previously, are behaviors (based upon group values and beliefs) that we practice so often that they become habitual. 'Norms that build trust, group identity, and group efficacy are the key to making teams click. They allow an otherwise highly-skilled and resourceful team to fulfill its potential, and they can help a team faced with substantial challenges achieve surprising victories.' (p89) As the old adage suggests, before a group can perform it must norm.

Norms for caring and for confrontation

In order for groups to manage relationships intelligently, they need to develop norms for caring and norms for confrontation. Most groups of teachers have little difficulty with norms for caring. These might include acknowledging the feelings of others, displaying positive regard, gestures and statements of appreciation, respectful behavior, support, validation and compassion.

Norms for confrontation are more problematic. First we need to acknowledge the fact that highly intelligent groups *do* engage in confrontation. We wrote earlier that one feature of organizational intelligence is cognitive conflict – confrontation, respectfully handled, that is focused on issues or ideas – not on the personality of the other person.

Norms for confrontation need to be deliberately and explicitly developed by the group as part of the team's essential agreements. How will we express our disagreement without derailing the group process? How do we rope in a colleague who is dominating the conversation or pursuing a personal, unrelated agenda? How will we remind a team member that he or she isn't following the rules?

Norms can come from a number of different sources, from formal and informal team leadership (the chair of committee or the convener of a task force); from courageous followers who ask naïve questions ("Is this a matter of principle or procedure?" "Help me to understand how this is related to our goal?"); through training; or from the cultural values of the larger organization (Druskat & Wolff, 2001).

Climate change

The bottom line is that any effort to enhance collective intelligence is bound to fail unless it also improves the quality of relationships within the organization. While is it difficult to argue against the veracity of the previous sentence, it is extremely easy to ignore it. This is perhaps the greatest dilemma facing schools.

Many good schools have come to resemble pressure cookers. There is a climate of dynamic change, turbulence, in some cases competition, where stressed teachers and students desperately try to find enough time in the day to complete all that is required of them (or that they have come to require of themselves). This is not the school climate that fosters sustained reflection or professional learning.

Teachers and school leaders must step back from the day-to-day focus of getting more done, of striving after 'results' and carve out sacred time for personal and group development. This involves climate change, perhaps the most complex of all adaptive challenges.

Reflection and transformational learning may seem an unaffordable luxury or a 'soft option' in today's fast-paced and results-oriented environment, but without time spent on these essential activities schools will not become smarter, more intelligent places.

References

Albrecht, K. (2003). *The Power of Minds at Work: Organizational Intelligence in Action.* New York: American Management Association.

Anderson, L. W., & David R. Krathwohl, D. R., et al (Eds.) (2001) *A Taxonomy for Learning, Teaching, and Assessing: A Revision of Bloom's Taxonomy of Educational Objectives.* Boston: Allyn & Bacon (Pearson Education Group).

Bandler, R., Grinder, J. (1979). *Frogs into Princes: Neuro Linguistic Programming.* Moab, UT: Real People Press.

Barber, M., Fenton, W., & Clark, M. (2010). *Capturing the Leadership Premium: How the world's top school systems are building leadership capacity for the future.* McKinsey & Company, retrieved from http://mckinseyonsociety.com/downloads/reports/Education/schoolleadership_final.pdf

Baron-Cohen, S. (2003). *The Essential Difference: Men, women and the extreme male brain.* London: Penguin.

Barth, R. (2006). Improving Relationships Within the Schoolhouse. *Educational Leadership, 63*(6), 8-13.

Barth, R. (1990). *Improving Schools from Within.* San Francisco: Jossey-Bass.

Bloom B. S. (1956). *Taxonomy of Educational Objectives, Handbook I: The Cognitive Domain.* New York: David McKay Co. Inc.

Brown, J. & Issacs, D. (2005). *The World Café: Shaping our Futures Through Conversations that Matter.* San Francisco: Berrett-Koehler Publishers.

Bryk, A.S. & Scneider, B. (2005). *Trust in schools: A core resource for improvement.* New York: Russell Sage Foundation.

Chappuis, J. (2005). Helping Students Understand Assessment. *Educational Leadership, 63*(3), 39-43.

Cherniss, C. & Goleman, D. (2001). *The Emotionally Intelligent Workplace.* San Francisco: Jossey Bass.

Cohen, E. G. & Lotan, R. A. (1997). *Working for equity in heterogeneous classrooms: Sociological theory in practice.* New York: Teachers College Press.

Collins, J. (2001). *From good to great: Why some companies make the leap...and others don't.* London: Random House.

Cook, L., & Friend, M. (1991). Principles for the Practice of Collaboration in Schools. *Preventing School Failure, 35*(4), 6-9.

Costa, A. & Garmston, R. (2002). *Cognitive Coaching: A Foundation for Renaissance Schools, 2nd Edition.* Norwood, MA.: Christopher Gordon Publisher.

Covey, S. (2004). *The Seven Habits of Highly Effective People.* London: Simon & Schuster.

de Bono, E. (1991). *I Am Right, You Are Wrong: From This to the New Renaissance: From Rock Logic to Water Logic.* London: Penguin.

Dilts, R. B. (1994). *Effective Presentation Skills.* Capitola, CA: Meta.

De Geus, A. (1997). *The Living Company.* Boston: Harvard Business School Press.

Drago-Severson, E. (2009). *Leading adult learning: Supporting adult development in our schools.* Thousand Oaks, CA: Corwin Press.

Druskat, *V. U. &* Wolff, S. B. (2001). Building the emotional intelligence of groups. *Harvard Business Review*,79(3), 81-90.

Dufour, R., & Eaker, R. (1998). *Professional learning communities at work: Best practices for enhancing student achievement.* Bloomington, IN: National Educational Service.

Duncan, W. (2007). *Strategic intuition: The creative spark in human achievement.* New York : Columbia University Press.

Dweck, C. S. (2008). *Mindsets: The new psychology of success.* New York: Ballantine Books.

Ellmore, R. F. (2000). *Building a new structure for school leadership.* Washington DC: The Albert Shanker Institute.

Erikson, E. H. (1973). *Childhood and society.* London: Penguin.

Fisher, D. & Frey, N. (2012). Making time for feedback. *Educational Leadership, 70(1),* 42 – 46.

Flinn, S.D. (2010). *The learning layer: Building the next level of intellect on your organization.* New York: Palgrave Macmillan.

Fredrickson, B.L., & Losada, M. F. (2005). Positive affect and complex dynamics of human flourishing. *American Psychologist,* 60 (7), 678-686.

Fullan, M. (2000). Conference presentation at The Academy of International School Heads, Washington DC, July 2000.

Fullan, M. (2001). *Leading in a Culture of Change.* San Francisco: Jossey-Bass.

Fullan, M. (2010). *All systems go: The change imperative for whole system Reform.* Thousand Oaks, CA: Corwin.

Fullan, M. (2011). *Change leader: Learning to do what matters most.* San Francisco: John Wiley & Sons.

Garmston, R. (2012). *Unlocking group potential to improve schools.* Thousand Oaks, CA: Corwin.

Garmston, R. (2005). *The presenter's fieldbook.* Norwood, MA: Christopher Gordon Publishers.

Garmston, R. & Wellman, B. (1998). Teacher Talk that Makes a Difference. *Educational Leadership, 55(7),* 30-34.

Garmston, R. & Wellman, B. (2009). *The adaptive school: A sourcebook for developing collaborative groups.* Norwood, MA: Christopher Gordon Publishers.

Goleman, D. (1985). *Emotional intelligence: Why it can matter more than IQ.* New York: Bantam Books.

Harris, Louis Associates. (2000). *The Spherion Report: Understanding emerging workforce trends.*

Hattie, J. (2012). Know thy impact. *Educational Leadership, 70(1),*18-23.

Hattie, J. (2009). *Visible learning: A synthesis of over 800 meta-analyses relating to achievement.* New York: Routledge.

Hatfield, E., Cacioppo, J. T., & Rapson, R. L. (1994). *Emotional contagion.* New York: Cambridge University Press.

Heifetz, R. A., & Linsky, M. (2002). *Leadership on the line: Staying alive through the dangers of leading.* Cambridge, MA: Harvard Business School Press.

Iacaboni, M. (2009). *Mirroring people: The science of empathy and how we connect with others.* New York: Picador Books.

Janis, I. L. (1972). *Victims of groupthink: A psychological study of foreign-policy decisions and fiascoes.* Boston: Houghton Mifflin.

Johnson, B. (1996). *Polarity management: Identifying and managing unsolvable problems.* Amherst, MA: HRD Press.

Jonsson, P. (2012). Lifeguard fired for saving man outside his zone. *Christian Science Monitor,* July 5, 2012.

Keats, J. (1899). *The complete poetical works and letters of John Keats, Cambridge Edition.* New York: Houghton, Mifflin and Company.

Kegan, R. (1994). *In over our heads: The mental demands of modern life.* Cambridge, MA: Harvard University Press

Kegan, R. & Lahey, L.L. (2009). *Immunity to change: How to overcome it and unlock the potential in yourself and your organization.* Boston, MA: Harvard Business Press.

Kluger, A. N., & DeNisi, A. (1996). The effects of feedback interventions on performance: A historical review, a meta-analysis, and a preliminary feedback intervention theory. *Psychological Bulletin, 119(2),* 254-284.

Knox, R. (1998). *The 80/20 principle: The secret to achieving more with less.* New York: Doubleday.

Koestler, A. (1990). *The ghost in the machine, Reprinted Edition.* London: Hutchinson.

Kreitner, R. & Kinicki, A. (2010). *Organizational behavior, 9th Edition.* New York: McGraw-Hill.

Kusuma-Powell, O. & Powell, W. (2000). *Count Me In! Developing Inclusive International Schools.* Washington DC: Office of Overseas Schools, US Department of State.

Lambert, L. (1998). *Building leadership capacity in schools.* Alexandria, VA: Association for Supervision and Curriculum Development.

Lefcourt H.M. (1982). *Locus of control.* Hillsdale, NJ: Lawrence Erlbaum.

Lipton, L. & Wellman, B. (2013). Creating communities of thought: Skills, tasks and practices. In *The Power of the Social Brain,* Arthur L. Costa and Pat Wilson, Editors. New York: Teachers College Press.

Lortie, D. (1975). *School teacher: A sociological study.* Chicago: University of Chicago Press.

Losado, M., & Heaphy, E. (2004). The role of positivity and connectivity in performance of business teams: A nonlinear dynamic model. *American Behavioral Scientist, 47(6),* 740-765.

Marzano, R., Pickering, D. & Pollock, J. (2001). *Classroom instruction that works.* Alexandria, VA: Association for Supervision and Curriculum Development.

Maslow, A (1954). *Motivation and personality.* New York: Harper.

Montgomery, D. (1989). *The fall of the house of labor: The workplace, the state, and American labor activism, 1865-1925.* Cambridge, MA: Cambridge University Press.

Mourshed, M., Chinezi, C, & Barber, M. (2010). *How the world's most improved school systems keep getting better.* McKinsey & Company, retrieved from http://mckinseyonsociety.com/downloads/reports/Education/How-the-Worlds-Most-Improved-School-Systems-Keep-Getting-Better_Download-version_Final.pdf

Nisbett, R. (2009). *Intelligence and how to get it: Why schools and culture Counts.* New York: W.W. Norton & Company.

Orlando Sentinel (1998). Student suspended for wine gift back in school, *Orlando Sentinel,* January 17, 1998.

Pascale, R., Sternin, J. & Sternin, M. (2010). *The power of positive deviance: How unlikely innovators solve the world's toughest problems.* Boston, MA: Harvard Business School Publishing.

Pelletier,K., Bartlett, K., Powell, W., & Kusuma-Powell, O. (2012). *The Next Frontier Inclusion: A Practical Guide for International School Leaders.* Next Frontier: Inclusion.

Perkins, D. (2003). *King Arthur's round table: How collaborative conversations create smart organizations. Hoboken, NJ:* John Wiley & Sons.

Pfeffer, J. & Sutton, R. I., (2006). *Hard facts, dangerous half truths, & total nonsense.* Boston, MA: Harvard Business School Publishing.

Piaget, J. (1957). *Construction of reality in the child.* London: Routledge & Kegan Paul.

Pink, D. (2009). *Drive: The surprising truth about what motivates us.* New York: Riverhead Books.

Powell, W. & Kusuma-Powell, O. (2010). *Becoming an emotionally intelligent teacher.* Thousand Oaks, CA: Corwin.

Powell, W. & Kusuma-Powell, O. (2011). *How to teach now: Five keys to personalized learning in the global classroom.* Alexandria, VA: Association for Supervision and Curriculum Development.

Rattan, A. Good, C. & Dweck, C. (2012). It's OK—Not everyone can be good at math. *Journal of Experimental Social Psychology, 48(2012),* 731 – 737, retrieved from https://www.asms.sa.edu.au/wp-content/uploads/2013/04/Dweck-article-on-mindset.pdf

Ritchart, R., Church, M., & Morrison, K. (2011). *Making thinking visible.* San Francisco: Jossey-Bass.

Rooke, D. & Torbet, W.R. (2005). Seven transformations of leadership. *Harvard Business Review.*

Sanford, C. (1995). The Myths of Organizational Effectiveness. *At Work, Sept/Oct,* 10-12.

Sawyer, K. (2007). *Group genius: The creative power of collaboration.* New York: Basic Books.

Seashore-Louis, K., Marks, H. & Kruse, S. (1995). Teachers' professional

community in restructuring schools. U.S. Dept. of Education, Office of Educational Research and Improvement, Educational Resources Information Center.

Senge, P. (2012). *Schools that learn.* New York: Crown Publishing.

Spillane, J.P., & Sherer, J. Z. (2004). A distributed perspective on leadership: leadership practice as stretched over people and place. Paper presented at the American Educational Research Association, Institute of Policy Research, Northwestern University, Evanston IL.

Spillaine, J.P., Halverson, R. & Diamond, J.B. (2004). Towards a theory of leadership practice: A distributed perspective. *Journal of Curriculum Studies, 36(1),* 3-34.

Symington, J. & Symington, N. (1996). *The clinical thinking of Wilfrid Bion.* Oxford, UK: Routledge.

Tschannen-Moran, M. (2004) *Trust matters: Leadership for Successful Schools.* San Francisco: Jossey-Bass.

Thompson, M. (2004). Can Narrative Therapy Heal the School Family. *Independent School,* National Association of Independent Schools, retrieved from www.nais.org/Articles/Pages/Can-Narrative-Therapy-Heal-the-School-Family-Part-I.aspx

Tomlinson, C. A. (2003). Deciding to teach them all. *Educational Leadership, 61(2)*, 6 – 11.

Tuchman, B. (1962). *The proud tower: A portrait of the world before World War One, 1980-1914.* New York: Ballantine Books.

Tuchman, B. (1962). *The guns of August.* New York: The MacMillan Company.

Tuchman, B (1984). *The march of folly: From Troy to Vietnam.* New York: Ballantine Books.

Unger, R. (2004). *False necessity: Anti-necessitarian social theory in the service of radical democracy, Revised Edition (Politics, Vol. 1).* London: Verso.

Van der Heijden, K. (2002). *The sixth sense: Accelerating organizational learning with scenarios.* Chichester, UK: John Wiley & Sons.

Vygotsky, L. (1986). *Thought and language.* Cambridge, MA: The Massachusetts Institute of Technology.

Wellman, B. (2013). Conference presentation, Thinking Collaborative Symposium, Denver, CO. January 23rd, 2013.

Wheatley, M. (2006). *Leadership and the new science: Discovering order in a chaotic world.* San Francisco: Berrett-Koehler Publishers.

White, M. and Epston, D. (1990). *Narrative means to therapeutic ends.* New York: W. W. Norton.

Wiggins, G. (2012). Seven keys to effective feedback. *Educational Leadership, 70(1)*, 11-16.

Wiggins, G. & McTighe, J. (2005) *Understanding by design, Expanded 2nd Edition.* Alexandria, VA: Association for Supervision and Curriculum Development.

Wiliam, D. (2012). Feedback: Part of a System. *Educational Leadership 70(1)*, 31-34.

Woolley, A.W., Chabris, C.F., Pentland, A., Hashmi, N., & Malone, T.W. (2010). Evidence for a Collective Intelligence Factor in the Performance of Human Groups. Published Online September 30 2010. *Science* 29 October 2010: Vol. 330 no. 6004 pp. 686-688. DOI: 10.1126/science.1193147

Woolley, A.W., & Malone, T.W. (2011). Defend your research: What makes a team smarter? More women. *Harvard Business Review, 89(6)*, 32-33.

Zimbardo, P. & Boyd, J. (2008). *The time paradox: The new psychology of time that will change your life.* New York: Free Press.

Zupkin, A. (2000). The Wisdom of Thoughtfulness. *New York Times,* May 31, 2000.